teacher's friend
publications

April!

a creative idea book
for the
elementary teacher

written and illustrated
by
Karen Sevaly

Copyright © Teacher's Friend,
a Scholastic Company
All rights reserved.
Printed in the U.S.A.

ISBN-13 978-0439-50373-0
ISBN-10 0-439-50373-6

This book is dedicated
to teachers and children
everywhere.

Table of Contents

Making the most of it!

7

WHAT IS IN THIS BOOK:

You will find the following in each monthly idea book from Teacher's Friend Publications:

1. A calendar listing every day of the month with classroom ideas and mention of special holidays and events.

2. At least four student awards to be sent home to parents.

3. Three or more bookmarks that can be used in your school library or given to students by you as "Super Student Awards."

4. Numerous bulletin board ideas and patterns pertaining to the particular month and seasonal activity.

5. Easy-to-make craft ideas related to the monthly holidays and special days.

6. Dozens of activities emphasizing not only the obvious holidays, but also the other celebrations such as the Olympics and Arbor Day.

7. Creative writing pages, crossword puzzles, word finds, booklet covers, games, paperbag puppets, literature lists and much more!

8. Scores of classroom management techniques and methods proven to motivate your students to improve behavior and classroom work.

HOW TO USE THIS BOOK:

Every page of this book may be duplicated for individual classroom use.

Some pages are meant to be copied or used as duplicating masters. Other pages may be transferred onto construction paper or used as they are.

If you have access to a print shop, you will find that many pages work well when printed on index paper. This type of paper takes crayons and felt markers well and is sturdy enough to last. (Bookmarks work particularly well on index paper.)

Lastly, some pages are meant to be enlarged with an overhead or opaque projector. When we say enlarge, we mean it! Think BIG! Three, four or even five feet is great! Try using colored butcher paper or posterboard so you don't spend all your time coloring.

MONTHLY ORGANIZERS:

Staying organized month after month, year after year can be a real challenge. Try this simple idea:

After using the loose pages from this book, file them in their own file folder labeled with the month's name. This will also provide a place to save pages from other reproducible books along with craft ideas, recipes and articles you find in magazines. (*Essential Pocket Folders* by Teacher's Friend provide a perfect way to store your monthly ideas and reproducibles. Each *Monthly Essential Pocket Folder* comes with a sixteen-page booklet of essential patterns and organizational ideas. There are even special folders for *Back to School*, *The Substitute Teacher* and *Parent-Teacher Conferences*.)

You might also like to dedicate a file box for every month of the school year. A covered box will provide room to store large patterns, sample art projects, certificates and awards, monthly stickers, monthly idea books and much more.

BULLETIN BOARDS IDEAS:

Creating clever bulletin boards for your classroom need not take fantastic amounts of time and money. With a little preparation and know-how, you can have different boards each month with very little effort. Try some of these ideas:

1. Background paper should be put up only once a year. Choose colors that can go with many themes and holidays. The black butcher-paper background you used as a spooky display in October will have a special dramatic effect in April with student-made, paper-cut butterflies.

2. Butcher paper is not the only thing that can be used to cover the back of your board. You might also try fabric from a colorful bed sheet or gingham material. Just fold it up at the end of the year to reuse again. Wallpaper is another great background cover. Discontinued rolls can be purchased for a small amount at discount hardware stores. Most can be wiped clean and will not fade like construction paper. (Do not glue wallpaper directly to the board; just staple or pin in place.)

3. Store your bulletin board pieces in large, flat envelopes made from two large sheets of tagboard or cardboard. Simply staple three sides together and slip the pieces inside. (Small pieces can be stored in ziploc bags.) Label your large envelopes with the name of the bulletin board and the month and year you displayed it. Take a picture of each bulletin board display. Staple the picture to your storage envelope. Next year when you want to create the same display, you will know where everything goes. Kids can even follow your directions when you give them a picture to look at.

ADDING THE COLOR:

Putting the color to finished items can be a real bother to teachers in a rush. Try these ideas:

1. On small areas, watercolor markers work great. If your area is rather large, switch to crayons or even colored chalk or pastels.

    (Don't worry, lamination or a spray fixative will keep color on the work and off you. No laminator or fixative? A little hair spray will do the trick.)

2. The quickest method of coloring large items is to start with colored paper. (Posterboard, butcher paper or large construction paper work well.) Add a few dashes of a contrasting colored marker or crayon and you will have it made.

3. Try cutting character eyes, teeth, etc. from white typing paper and gluing them in place. These features will really stand out and make your bulletin boards come alive.

    For special effects, add real buttons or lace. Metallic paper looks great on stars and belt buckles, too.

LAMINATION:

If you have access to a roll laminator, then you already know how fortunate you are. They are priceless when it comes to saving time and money. Try these ideas:

1. You can laminate more than just classroom posters and construction paper. Try various kinds of fabric, wallpaper and giftwrap. You'll be surprised at the great combinations you come up with.

    Laminated classified ads can be used to cut headings for current events bulletin boards. Colorful gingham fabric makes terrific cut letters or bulletin board trim. You might even try burlap! Bright foil giftwrap will add a festive feeling to any bulletin board.

    (You can even make professional looking bookmarks with laminated fabric or burlap. They are great holiday gift ideas for Mom or Dad!)

2. Felt markers and laminated paper or fabric can work as a team. Just make sure the markers you use are permanent and not water-based. Oops, made a mistake! That's okay. Put a little ditto fluid on a tissue, rub across the mark and presto, it's gone! Also, dry transfer markers work great on lamination and can easily be wiped off.

LAMINATION:
(continued)

3. Laminating cut-out characters can be tricky. If you have enlarged an illustration onto posterboard, simply laminate first and then cut it out with scissors or an art knife. (Just make sure the laminator is hot enough to create a good seal.)

One problem may arise when you paste an illustration onto posterboard and laminate the finished product. If your paste-up is not 100% complete, your illustration and posterboard may separate after laminating. To avoid this problem, paste your illustration onto posterboard that measures slightly larger than the illustration. This way, the lamination will help hold down your paste-up.

4. When pasting-up your illustration, always try to use either rubber cement, artist's spray adhesive or a glue stick. White glue, tape or paste does not laminate well because it can often be seen under your artwork.

5. Have you ever laminated student-made place mats, crayon shavings, tissue paper collages, or dried flowers? You'll be amazed at the variety of creative things that can be laminated and used in the classroom or as take-home gifts.

PHOTOCOPIES AND DITTO MASTERS:

Many of the pages in this book can be copied for use in the classroom. Try some of these ideas for best results:

1. If the print from the back side of your original comes through the front when making a photocopy or ditto master, slip a sheet of black construction paper behind the sheet. This will mask the unwanted shadows and create a much better copy.

2. Several potential masters in this book contain instructions for the teacher. Simply cover the type with correction fluid or a small slip of paper before duplicating.

3. When using a new ditto master, turn down the pressure on the duplicating machine. As the copies become light, increase the pressure. This will get longer wear out of both the master and the machine.

4. Trying to squeeze one more run out of that worn ditto master can be frustrating. Try lightly spraying the inked side of the master with hair spray. For some reason, this helps the master put out those few extra copies.

LETTERING AND HEADINGS:

Not every school has a letter machine that produces perfect 4" letters. The rest of us will just have to use the old stencil-and-scissor method. But wait, there is an easier way!

1. Don't cut individual letters because they are difficult to pin up straight. Instead, hand print bulletin board titles and headings onto strips of colored paper. When it is time for the board to come down, simply roll it up to use again next year. If you buy your own pre-cut lettering, save yourself some time and hassle by pasting the desired statements onto long strips of colored paper. Laminate if possible. These can be rolled up and stored the same way!

    Use your imagination! Try cloud shapes and cartoon bubbles. They will all look great.

2. Hand-lettering is not that difficult, even if your printing is not up to penmanship standards. Print block letters with a felt marker. Draw big dots at the end of each letter. This will hide any mistakes and add a charming touch to the overall effect.

    If you are still afraid to freehand it, try this nifty idea: Cut a strip of poster board about 28" X 6". Down the center of the strip, cut a window with an art knife measuring 20" X 2". There you have it: a perfect stencil for any lettering job. All you need to do is write capital letters with a felt marker within the window slot. Don't worry about uniformity. Just fill up the entire window height with your letters. Move your posterboard strip along as you go. The letters will always remain straight and even because the posterboard window is straight.

3. If you must cut individual letters, use construction paper squares measuring 4 1/2" X 6". (Laminate first if you can.) Cut the capital letters as shown. No need to measure; irregular letters will look creative and not messy.

Calendar

April

APRIL

1ST Today is APRIL FOOL'S DAY! (As a creative writing assignment, have your students write about a harmless trick they might pull on a friend.)

2ND HANS CHRISTIAN ANDERSEN, famous Danish author, was born on this day in 1805. (Read one of his stories to your class.) Today is also INTERNATIONAL CHILDREN'S BOOK DAY!

3RD Today marks the birthday of WASHINGTON IRVING, famous American author. (Introduce your students to two of his characters, Rip Van Winkle and Ichabod Crane.)

4TH On this day in 1949, the NORTH ATLANTIC TREATY ORGANIZATION was formed. (Ask students to find out the purpose of this organization.)

5TH BOOKER T. WASHINGTON, one of the foremost educators and leaders of African Americans, was born on this day in 1856. (Ask students to find out more about this man.)

6TH The first modern OLYMPIC GAMES were held in Athens, Greece, on this day in 1896. (Organize your own Academic Olympics with such events as "Marathon Math" and "Gold Medal Spelling.")

7TH Today is WORLD HEALTH DAY! (Lead your students in a set of "jumping jacks" and "toe touches." Tell them about the importance of exercise and taking care of their bodies.)

8TH Spanish explorer PONCE DE LEON reached the eastern coast of North America on this day in 1513. (Trace his route on the classroom map.)

9TH America's first free, tax-supported PUBLIC LIBRARY opened its doors on this day in 1833 in Peterborough, New Hampshire. (Arrange a field trip to the nearest public library in honor of this day.)

10TH Nebraska celebrated the first ARBOR DAY by planting 10 million trees throughout the state in 1872. (Celebrate your own Arbor Day by planting a tree on the school grounds.)

11TH JACKIE ROBINSON became the first black Major League baseball player on this day in 1947. (Ask students to find out more about the early days of American baseball.)

12TH Soviet cosmonaut YURI GAGARIN became the first man in space on this day in 1961. (Ask students to research America's space program and Alan Shepard, Jr., the first American astronaut.

13TH Today marks the birthday of America's third PRESIDENT. (He was born in 1743 and his picture appears on every nickel. Have your students guess his name.)

14TH The first edition of WEBSTER'S AMERICAN DICTIONARY was published on this day in 1828. (Give your students a list of "fun" words to define using the dictionary.)

15TH The luxury liner "TITANIC" sank on its maiden voyage on this day in 1912. (Ask students to find out what made this great ship go down.)

16TH Today marks the anniversary of the BOSTON MARATHON. (Demonstrate to your students the distance of 26 miles by comparing points of interest around town.)

17TH Italian explorer GIOVANNI DA VERRAZANO discovered what was later called New York Harbor on this day in 1524. (Ask a student to locate the harbor on the class map.)

18TH American patriot PAUL REVERE completed his famous ride to warn of the British invasion on this day in 1775. (Read to your class the poem "Paul Revere's Ride" by Henry Wadsworth Longfellow.)

19TH Today is PATRIOT'S DAY, commemorating the Battle of Lexington and the beginning of the American Revolution in 1775. (Lead your class in singing a patriotic song to celebrate.)

20TH DANIEL CHESTER FRENCH was born on this day in 1850. (Mr. French is famous for creating a well-known statue in Washington, DC. Ask students to find out which one.)

21ST FRIEDRICH FROEBEL, a German educator and founder of the first kindergarten, was born on this day in 1782. (Older students might like to volunteer to help in your school's kindergarten, reading a story or helping with a craft activity.)

22ND Today is EARTH DAY! (Celebrate this event by discussing ways to conserve our planet's resources and make it a better place to live.)

23RD Today marks the birthdate of WILLIAM SHAKESPEARE in 1564. (Discuss with your students this man's accomplishments and ask them to find a few quotes from his many plays.)

24TH The first American newspaper, THE BOSTON NEWS-LETTER, was published on this day in 1704. (Have students write a class newsletter that can be sent home to parents.)

25TH Construction of the SUEZ CANAL began on this day in 1859. (Ask students to find the canal on the classroom map and discuss the major reasons it was built.)

26TH JOHN JAMES AUDUBON, American naturalist and painter, was born on this day in 1785. (Celebrate his birthday by taking your class on a schoolground birdwatch.)

27TH Today marks the birthday of WALTER LANTZ, creator of Woody Woodpecker. (Ask students to create an original cartoon character with a special voice of its own.)

28TH Today is NATIONAL STUDENT LEADERSHIP DAY! (Have children take turns being class leaders throughout the day.)

29TH The United States' presence in VIETNAM came to an end on this day in 1975. (Older students might like to discuss their opinions of this war or other current international events.)

30TH On this day in 1789, GEORGE WASHINGTON was sworn in as the first president of the United States of America. (Ask students to find out how many presidents we have had since then.)

DON'T FORGET THESE OTHER IMPORTANT DAYS!

ARBOR DAY - This annual tree planting celebration is observed in most states during the month of April.

GOOD FRIDAY - On this day, Christians commemorate the day Jesus was convicted of treason and crucified. It is always observed on the Friday before Easter Sunday.

EASTER SUNDAY - This important Christian holiday celebrates the resurrection of Jesus Christ. Easter always falls on a Sunday between the dates of March 22nd and April 25th.

JEWISH PASSOVER - This important festival commemorates the exodus of the Jews from Egypt more than 3,000 years ago. Passover begins on the 14th day of the Jewish calendar month of Nisan.

TF0400 April Idea Book

April Calendar Symbols

April

Sunday	Monday	Tuesday	Wednesday	Thursday	Friday	Saturday

April Activities!

April Activities!

Say hello to the spring season by bringing to the classroom the sights and sounds of chirping chicks, blooming flowers and colorful gardens! Here are a few activities to get you started!

SPRINGTIME IN THE CLASSROOM

1. Have students make paper airplanes and conduct a contest to see which plane flies the farthest.
2. Select a variety of spring-related books from the school library and create a seasonal reading corner in your classroom complete with a flowering potted plant.
3. The next time your students seem especially restless, have them line up for a walk around the school grounds. Tell students to take notice of all the things they see that signal the signs of spring. Instruct students to list their springtime observations once they return to the classroom.
4. With the prediction of sunny weather, have your students bring their lunches to school for an outdoor picnic. You may want to provide a dessert of cupcakes or cookies for everyone in the class.
5. Divide the class into small groups and have them participate in an outdoor scavenger hunt. Each group can find and list such items as: four things that are green, three things that crawl, two things that fly, five things that grow, etc. Encourage the groups to share their findings with the class.
6. Have students collect a variety of materials that birds can use to build their spring nests. Short pieces of yarn, cotton balls, lint from the dryer and bits of tissue paper all work well. Place these items in a shallow cardboard box outside a classroom window. Students can watch the birds collect the bits and pieces to build their nests.

PLANTING MARIGOLDS

Marigolds are hardy flowers that can be easily grown from seeds in the classroom.

Give each student a small styrofoam cup and have them write their names on the cups with a permanent marker. Fill the cups half full with potting soil and let students place a couple of marigold seeds in the soil. Spoon more soil on top of the seeds and sprinkle with water. Place the cups in a sunny window. (Plant several additional cups just in case some don't sprout.)

Assign students to water the seeds every other day. As the plants grow, discuss with the students how plants need sunlight and water to grow. (You may want to place one plant in a dark closet. Ask students to observe if it grows as quickly as the ones in the sunlight.)

In a few weeks, the marigold plants will be large enough to take home--just in time for Mother's Day!

April Activities!

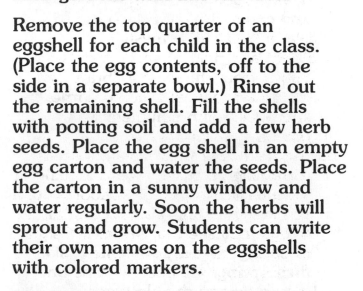

SPRING-FEVER SHOES

Students will have a fun time with this creative springtime art project! Have each student bring to class a worn pair of sneakers or shoes that are on the brink of being thrown away. You may want to visit yard sales to purchase additional pairs of shoes for use by your students.

Have children stuff the shoes with crumpled newspaper. Ask each student to draw a design on his or her shoes with a permanent marker. Now, have them paint the shoes with acrylic paints. When dry, have them add sequins, button, feathers, etc. with white glue. Declare a day to be "Spring-Fever Day" and have everyone wear their "new" shoes!

WILDFLOWERS

Ask students to collect a variety of wildflowers. Make sure to remind them not to pick flowers from parks or protected areas.

Ask students to identify the flowers they bring in by locating their descriptions in wildflower books. Press the wildflowers flat between sheets of newsprint with several heavy books. Once the wildflowers are dry, laminate them. The wildflowers can then be displayed on the class board with their names and descriptions.

Laminated wildflowers or common garden flowers, such as pansies, also make beautiful bookmarks. Trim the lamination in the shape of a bookmark, punch a hole at one end and attach a yarn tassel.

EGGSHELL HERB GARDENS

Students will love growing their own individual herb gardens with this fun idea.

Remove the top quarter of an eggshell for each child in the class. (Place the egg contents, off to the side in a separate bowl.) Rinse out the remaining shell. Fill the shells with potting soil and add a few herb seeds. Place the egg shell in an empty egg carton and water the seeds. Place the carton in a sunny window and water regularly. Soon the herbs will sprout and grow. Students can write their own names on the eggshells with colored markers.

The day after you plant the seeds, use the leftover egg mixture in a student cooking activity. Have the children carefully chop onion and bell pepper and add grated cheese to the mixture. Cook the omelet mixture in an electric skillet and give each student a small serving in a paper cup.

WHERE DO THEY GROW?

All fruits, vegetables, grains, nuts and beans are grown and harvested in different ways. Ask students to research a variety of these foods and determine how and where they are grown. Have them list five foods for each of these categories:

- FOODS GROWN ON TREES
- FOODS GROWN ON VINES
- FOODS GROWN ON PLANTS ABOVE GROUND
- FOODS GROWN BELOW GROUND

April Umbrella

Use the umbrella and raindrop patterns to create a matching activity. Label each section of the umbrella with math problems, contractions, ordinal numbers, etc. Cut the raindrops from colored paper and label each with the correct matching answer. Children match the raindrop to the appropriate problem.

24

TF0400 April Idea Book

What a Busy Bee!

_____
Student's Name

did a great job today!

_____
Teacher   Date

_____
Student's Name

did a super job today!

_____
Date

_____
Teacher

_____
Student's Name

was a joy in class today!

_____
Date

_____
Teacher

_____
Student's Name

worked hard today!

_____
Date

_____
Teacher

Pencil Toppers

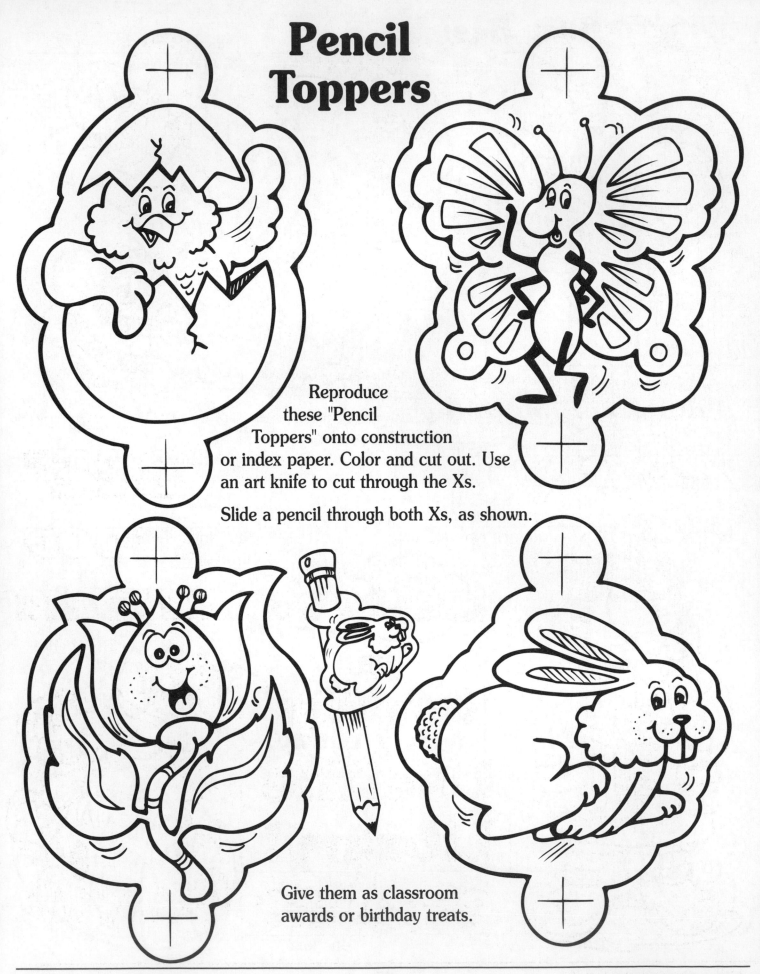

Reproduce these "Pencil Toppers" onto construction or index paper. Color and cut out. Use an art knife to cut through the Xs.

Slide a pencil through both Xs, as shown.

Give them as classroom awards or birthday treats.

A Book Can Be A Good Friend on a Rainy Day!

GROW in Knowledge! Use the Library!

"BEE" A GOOD READER!

27

TF0400 April Idea Book

April Booklet

FOLD

Name

TF0400 April Idea Book

CERTIFICATE of ACHIEVEMENT

presented to

NAME

in recognition of

TEACHER

DATE

STUDENT
OF THE
MONTH

NAME

SCHOOL

DATE

TEACHER

Rainy Day Writing!

31

Spring Color Page

April Fool's!

April Fool's Day Activities!

The first day of April is often called "All Fool's Day" or "April Fool's Day".

This fun-filled day may have been originally observed as part of the celebrations honoring the spring equinox when Mother Nature seems to "fool" us with her unpredictable weather! The French, however, can trace this silly day back to 1856 when changes were made to their calendar. Anyone who resisted the changes was tricked by pranksters and labeled an "April Fish!" Even now, on April 1st, French children try to attach paper fish to the backs of unsuspecting victims. If the person is fooled, he or she is then called an "April Fish!"

Try some of these silly but harmless activities with your students to motivate them into creative thinking and writing!

FOOLISH DRESS-UP DAY!

Announce to your students that April 1st will be "Foolish Dress-Up Day!" Encourage them to come to school dressed in a foolish way. Suggest that they wear clothes backward or inside-out, mismatched socks or shoes, funny hats and so on. As you take role in the morning, have each student stand and show off his or her "foolish" attire.

ALPHABET WRITING

Encourage creativity with this fun activity. Assign each student a letter of the alphabet. Ask students to write the longest sentence possible using only words beginning with their letter. (Small words such as *a, of, the,* etc. don't count.) Tell them that prizes will be awarded to the person with the silliest sentence and to the person with the longest sentence. Present the winners with a humorous prize like a dill pickle or a coupon to stay in at recess and work on a math assignment!

MIXED-UP NAMES

Before school starts on April 1st, write each student's name on a new name plate or name tag and arrange them so everyone will be sitting at a different desk. You may want to scramble the letters or reverse the syllables such as: Venste (Steven), Bertro (Robert) or Dalin (Linda). Encourage the students to use their new names all day!

April Fool's Day Activities!

CLASSROOM SCAVENGER HUNT

Select a number of unusual items from home and place them around the classroom for your students to locate. Give each student a list of the things you wish them to find. Write the list in a humorous way. Here are a few suggestions:

• A dentist's best friend! (toothbrush)
• To "bee" or not to "bee"! (jar of honey)
• "I can do it!" (can opener)
• No bones about it! (dog biscuit)

When time is up, declare the student with the most finds the winner. As a creative writing assignment, instruct students to write silly stories using the items they found on their lists.

TOSS AND CATCH

Reinforce eye-hand coordination and dexterity with this easy craft activity!

Collect enough large plastic bleach bottles or gallon milk cartons for each student in class. Cut off the bottom section of each bottle, leaving the handle intact. Children can decorate the bottles with permanent colored markers. Instruct the students to cut a 20-inch length of yarn and tie one end around the opening of the bottle, securing it with the plastic cap. Have them tie the other end of the yarn around a crumpled piece of aluminum foil.

The children can toss the "ball" and try to catch it in the bottle. Award a treat to the student who can "toss and catch" the most times in a row without missing.

FOOLISH PUPPETS

Instruct your students in making cute puppets for April Fool's Day.

Have them fold a sheet of construction paper into thirds, lengthwise and then into quarters where the ends meet in the middle. Tell them to reverse the folds so they can put their fingers into one slot and their thumbs in the other. They now have their puppet!

Encourage the children to decorate the puppet any way they wish with paper teeth, cotton-ball eyes, felt ears, etc. Students can use their puppet to recite nursery rhymes or riddles to other classmates.

Foolish Face

Give each student a copy of this face pattern. Have them draw a funny face and color with crayons.

Cut the faces along the dotted lines. Students can swap face sections and reassemble the "foolish faces."

A RIDDLE!

Write your favorite riddle on the question mark and its answer on the period. Cut out and have fellow classmates match the answer to the correct riddle!

Write Your Own Comic Strip!

Have you ever wanted to create your own comic strip? Here's your chance! Decide what your comic strip will be about and design your own characters. Many ideas in comic strips are communicated without words. Here are some common symbols and facial expressions. Write and draw your own comic strip on the comic strip pattern.

Symbols:

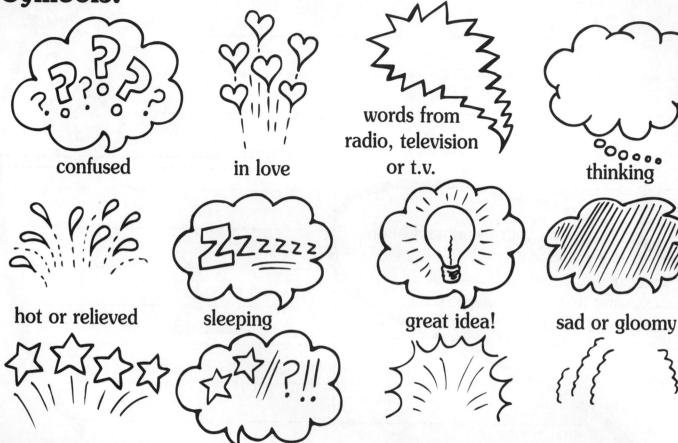

confused

in love

words from radio, television or t.v.

thinking

hot or relieved

sleeping

great idea!

sad or gloomy

dazed or knocked out

frustrated

shiny or bright

shivering or cold

Faces:

	Happy	Angry	Ill or Tired	Confused
Mouths				
Eyes and Eyebrows				

Put together the faces to look like this!

TF0400 April Idea Book

Jack-in-the-Box!

Copy these Jack-in-the-Box patterns onto heavy index paper and let the children do the coloring and cutting. Cut the four slits with a razor knife and insert the tabs through the slits. Jack's head can now be moved up and down.

Make a learning activity by writing a question or math problem on Jack's box and the answer on the spring. Children move Jack's head to reveal the correct answer.

Riddles can also be written on the boxes and funny answers on the springs! Display them on the class bulletin board.

TF0400 April Idea Book

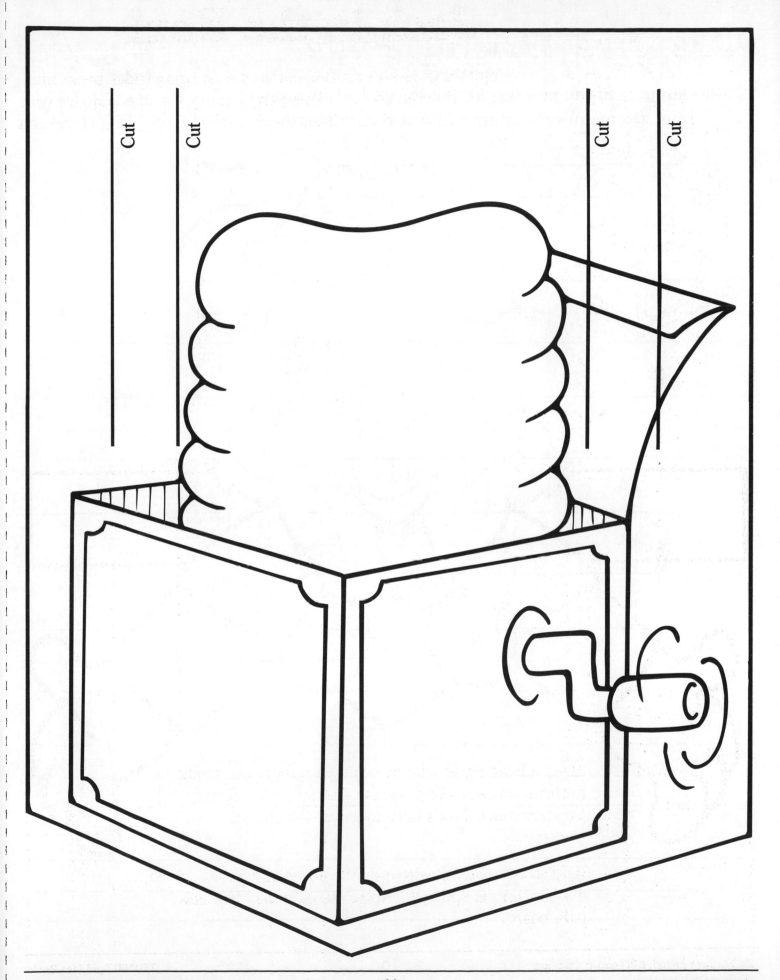

41

Creative Writing Page

Write about a prank you would like to play on someone
you know. (Remember: the prank must be harmless!)

Arbor Day!

Arbor Day Activities!

National Arbor Day is celebrated on the last Friday in April by most of the fifty states. The first Arbor Day celebrated in the United States was observed in Nebraska on April 22, 1872.

On Arbor Day, many schools and civic organizations plant a tree for the purpose of beautifying a neighborhood park or public area. The significance of planting a tree to honor special occasions is also customary in different cultures. "Arbor Day" is declared when the birth of a child takes place and a tree is planted in recognition. Try some of these activities in honor of Arbor Day!

PLANT A TREE

Several days before Arbor Day, arrange for your class to visit a local nursery that specializes in trees. (If a trip is not possible, then perhaps a local arborist can visit your classroom.) Those working at the nursery will be able to tell about the various trees and explain their care and climate needs. They will also be able to suggest a type of tree to plant for Arbor Day.

Purchase a sapling and take it back to the classroom. With the help of your students, plan a tree-planting ceremony. Children can design invitations that can be taken home to parents. Don't forget to invite the school principal and others.

On Arbor Day, plant your sapling in grand style with the help of each student. You may want to have students read tree poems or tell about how trees benefit us with their resources and beauty.

FAMILIAR TREES

Select between 10 or 20 trees found near or on your school campus. Mark the trees on a campus map and give each student a copy. Take your class on a nature walk and show them each of the trees. Children should take along the map and a notebook to record the information. Instruct them on each tree's individual name and its special characteristics. Point out each tree's unique shape, bark, leaves, color, etc.

After you return to class, have the children list each tree and organize the important information. When the students can truly identify the selected trees, have them take groups of younger students on the same nature walk. Your students will impress the youngsters with their knowledge about each tree and at the same time enrich their own love of trees and nature!

Arbor Day Activities!

ARBOR DAY FOOD FEAST

With the help of parents, supply a variety of foods that grow on trees for your students to sample. A sign-up sheet is provided below. Some suggestions are: almonds, apples, avocados, bananas, coconuts, lemons, oranges, pears, pecans, peaches, tangerines, walnuts, etc.

Parents will need to cut up the fruit for serving but students may enjoy using nutcrackers on almonds and walnuts.

Emphasize to your students that all of the foods were produced by trees. Have students rate which fruits or nuts are their favorites and which ones they might dislike.

TREE CARE

In 1872, the country's first Arbor Day was declared with the help of a man named J. Sterling Morton. He felt very strongly that all citizens needed to take a more active interest in the earth's natural resources, particularly its trees.

Ask students to list ways in which they can care for neighborhood trees and the environment in general. Students may like to "adopt" a tree on the school grounds or at a nearby park. They can care for the tree by picking up the litter around it, watering it during warm weather and/or placing mulch at the base of its trunk when the weather turns cold.

ARBOR DAY FOOD FEAST!

Dear Parents,

On _____, in celebration of Arbor Day, our class will be sampling the many foods that come from trees. Please help us by providing _____
_____.

Please feel free to attend. You can contact me at

_____.

Thank you!

_____
Teacher

_____
Room

Arbor Day Vine

Photocopy the leaf pattern onto green paper and distribute copies to students to cut out. Children can choose a tree in their own yard or nearby park to write about on the leaf. When the leaves are completed, students can attach the leaves to a long piece of green yarn by wrapping the stems around the yarn and gluing them in place.

Student's Name

Tree:

Age:

Location:

Height:

Interesting Facts:

My Arbor Day Book!

_____
Name

Reading Tree!

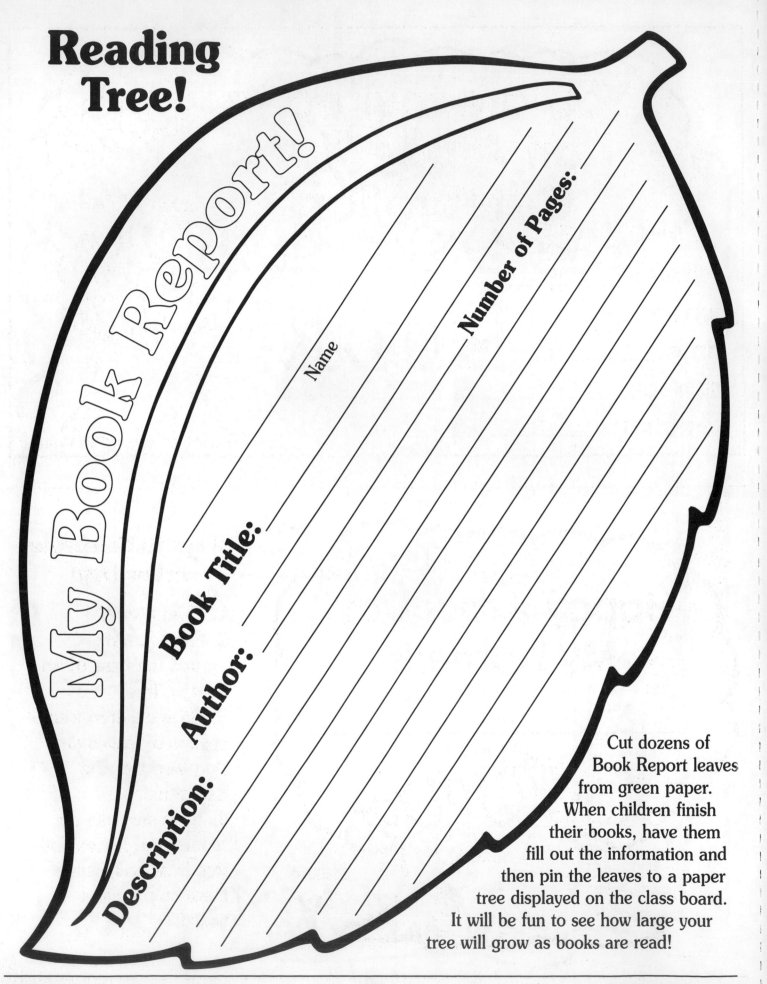

My Book Report!

Name

Number of Pages:

Book Title:

Author:

Description:

Cut dozens of Book Report leaves from green paper. When children finish their books, have them fill out the information and then pin the leaves to a paper tree displayed on the class board. It will be fun to see how large your tree will grow as books are read!

You are invited to an Arbor Day Celebration!

where: _____

when: _____

time: _____

school: _____

teacher: _____

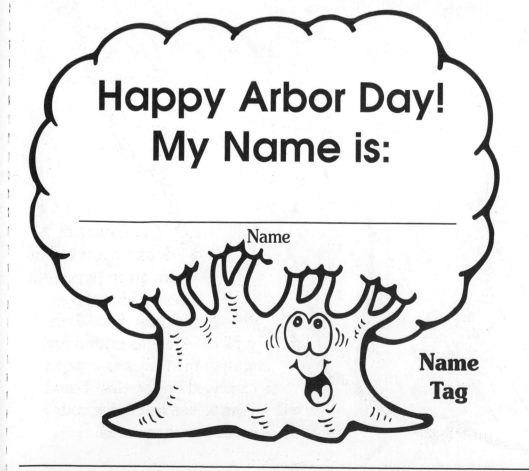

Happy Arbor Day! My Name is:

_____
Name

Name Tag

Ways to Celebrate Arbor Day!

1. Plant a tree.
2. Plant flowers around the base of an existing tree.
3. Have children wear crowns of leaves and sing "America the Beautiful."
4. Have students do rubbings of leaves and tree bark and display them on the class board.

Crown of Leaves

Make an Arbor Day Crown by stapling real leaves to a paper headband, or use these patterns cut from construction paper.

Earth Day!

Save the Earth Activities!

Celebrate Earth Day, April 22nd, and at the same time promote environmental awareness with these Save-the-Earth activities!

ENVIRONMENTAL NEWS

Ask students to collect articles and information about the earth's environment. Divide the class bulletin board and label each section with the headings air, land, water and animals.

Students can also collect the labels of products that claim recycled paper, biodegradable materials or species-safe products and display these on the class board.

RECYCLING FOR FUND RAISING

Encourage students to collect aluminum cans, plastic containers and glass bottles and jars as a class project. When a substantial quantity of recycled items have been collected, take them to a recycling center for reimbursement. With the money you have raised arrange for a class field trip. You may want to visit a business that uses recycled items to make new products, or tour a sewage treatment plant or recycling center.

ADOPT-A-CLEAN-TOWN

Some towns offer "Adopt-a-Street" or "Adopt-a-Park" programs. Inquire about programs your city might have to help promote graffiti and litter removal. With the help of parents, arrange for your students to volunteer to work cleaning up a park, beach or public area on a Saturday morning. Your students will be amazed at how much litter they can collect in just one morning.

PLANTS AND THE ENVIRONMENT

Demonstrate to your students how plants and trees give off oxygen which is essential to every person.

Plant several small plants in an aquarium or large plastic bottle. Make sure your plants are established in your new terrarium before doing this experiment.

Using a lighter or match, light a small scrap of paper and drop it into the terrarium, quickly sealing the top. The burning paper will create enough smoke to fill the container. Have your students observe what happens. The smoke will soon disappear and become clear. Explain to the children that plants and trees do the same in our environment. They absorb the smoky "dirty" air and replace it with oxygen.

Save the Earth Activities!

RANDOM ACTS OF ENVIRONMENTAL KINDNESS!

Encourage your students to practice one act of environmental kindness each day! Suggest some of the following:

- Pick up a piece of litter.
- Remind others not to litter.
- Water a tree or flower garden.
- Help your family recycle newspapers, cans and bottles.
- Conserve water by taking a shorter shower.
- Find ways to re-use papers and items that are usually thrown away.
- Don't be wasteful with food at meal time.
- Don't buy products that are not environmentally friendly.

Ask students to record their random acts and report on them at the end of the week.

ARTISTIC JUNK

Encourage your students to think of ways they can recycle clean throwaways in artistic ways! Plan a day in which they can make these fun crafts from the things they have collected from home. Here are some ideas:

EGG CARTONS

- Make a seedling planter by using the paper type of egg carton. Fill each section with potting soil and plant with flower, vegetable or herb seeds. After the plants have sprouted, cut the sections apart and plant them directly into the soil outside.
- Cut the egg carton sections apart and make insect crafts such as ladybugs, caterpillars and butterflies.
- Make pretty spring flowers by cutting the styrofoam section of the egg cartons apart. Trim the sections into the shapes of flower petals. Attach the sections to pipe cleaners and add green paper leaves.

NEWSPAPERS

- Make papier-mâché from torn newspapers and wallpaper paste. Have kids cover blown balloons with the papier-mâché. When dry, they can be painted with poster paints.
- Make fireplace logs by rolling newspapers very tightly and securing them with string.

MILK CARTONS

- Pencil holders can be made by cutting the tops off small milk cartons and covering them with colored paper. Kids can decorate the holders any way they choose.
- Make a bird feeder by cutting an opening in one side of a milk carton. Insert a popsicle stick for a perch and fill with birdseed. Attach a string to the top and hang in a tree.

PAPER ROLLS

- Make napkin rings from two-inch sections of a toiletpaper roll or papertowel roll. Children can wrap colorful yarn around the sections to make the napkin rings.
- A music kazoo can be made with a toiletpaper roll, a square of waxed paper and a rubber band. Place the waxed paper over one end of the roll and attach with the rubber band. Children can decorate the roll and blow through the open end to play the kazoo.

PLASTIC CONTAINERS

- Plastic margarine tubs can be used to make hanging planters or desk organizers.

Environmental Acts of Kindness Pledge!

I pledge to perform random acts of environmental kindness each day by finding ways to conserve water, materials and energy. I also promise to help keep the earth a beautiful and safe place to live by not littering, writing graffiti or being wasteful.

_____   _____
Student's Signature   **Date**

Name _____

RANDOM ACTS of ENVIRONMENTAL KINDNESS

"I promise to do my best to keep the earth beautiful and safe by not littering, writing graffiti or causing being wasteful."

Ask students to read the Environmental Acts of Kindness pledge aloud and then date and sign it. Post the pledges on the class board as a reminder to students of ways they can care for the earth.

Have the students record their acts of environmental kindness and wear this name tag home to encourage family members to become involved.

Student's Name _____

Random Acts of Environmental Kindness!

Here are the ways I found to promote environmental kindness!

Sunday _____

_____
Date

Monday _____

_____
Date

Tuesday _____

_____
Date

Wednesday _____

_____
Date

Thursday _____

_____
Date

Friday _____

_____
Date

Saturday _____

_____
Date

Environmental Kindness Parent Letter

Dear Parents,

   In recognition of Earth Day, our class is striving to be good citizens by finding ways we can help improve and protect the earth and the environment in which we live. As part of this effort, students are pledging to *"practice random acts of environmental kindness"* each day. Here are some ways you can help:

• Provide recycling containers in your home for aluminum, paper, plastic and glass. Take the items to a recycling center or use curbside pickup if it is provided in your neighborhood.

• Re-use items such as grocery sacks, plastic bags, glass jars, boxes and plastic containers whenever possible.

• Be a good example to your child by disposing litter appropriately and encouraging him or her to do the same.

• Reduce the use of disposable products by using items that can be washed and reused such as glasses and dishes instead of paper plates and cups or cloth towels instead of papertowels.

• Stress the importance of respecting your neighborhood by never defacing walls, buildings, trees, etc. with grafitti.

• Conserve energy by turning lights off when you leave a room and turning down the heat at night. Encourage your child to do the same.

I truly appreciate your support and cooperation concerning the education of your child.

                              Sincerely,

Earth First!
Visor

Copy this visor onto sturdy index or construction paper. Children can do the coloring.

Punch holes at both ends and attach string elastic. (With elastic, the students can easily remove the visor without retying.)

If you wish to save on the cost of elastic, simply use mailing string. Either way, the kids will love them and so will you!

EARTH FIRST!

"I pledge to practice random acts of environmental kindness every day!"

My Family's Recycling Report

Student's Name

These things are regularly recycled by my family:

☐ aluminum cans   ☐ yard waste

☐ newspapers   ☐ cardboard/boxes

☐ plastic   ☐ clothing (donated or handed down)

☐ glass   ☐ grocery bags

☐ magazines   ☐ _____

We also take extra care in disposing of paints, chemicals, used automobile oil, etc. in this way:

_____

_____

_____

The reasons we recycle: **The reasons we don't recycle:**

My thoughts: _____

Name

MY GARBAGE CAN STORY

Name

Easter!

The Easter Holiday!

In many countries around the world, Easter signifies the birth of spring. It is a time of fairs, festivals, parades and Christian celebrations. Many people dress in fancy new clothes for Easter Sunday and many cities sponsor special Easter parades. Many symbols are associated with Easter Sunday. Here are a few favorites.

EASTER EGGS

The Persians believed that the egg symbolized life and that the earth was hatched from a giant egg. In the Slavic countries of Europe, people have handpainted intricate designs on Easter eggs for centuries. The eggs are then given as gifts of love and admiration, like valentines.

Today, many communities hold Easter egg hunts. The eggs are hidden in local parks, backyards or meadows. Children of all ages hunt for the eggs. At most egg hunts, the person who finds the most eggs wins a prize. One of the most famous Easter egg hunts takes place every year on the lawn of the White House, usually on the Saturday before Easter.

EASTER RABBIT

There are many opinions on the origin of the Easter rabbit. In the ancient world, the hare was considered a symbol of fertility and stood for the rebirth of life, associated with spring. Some Asian cultures consider the hare a symbol of the moon. This idea may have encouraged the concept of the Easter rabbit because the moon determines the date of Easter.

The legend of the "Easter bunny" who brings colored eggs on Easter morning probably came from a story told in Germany. It is said that long ago, during a famine, a poor woman dyed a few eggs and hid them in a nest as Easter gifts for her children. Just as the children discovered the eggs, a large rabbit was seen hopping away. The story of the "bunny" grew until it finally became the tale of the Easter bunny.

HOT-CROSS BUNS

During the six weeks of Lent, hot-cross buns are available in most bakeries. The serving of these buns was probably a tradition passed down from ancient Anglo-Saxons. They prepared special baked goods in honor of "Eastore" the goddess of spring and fertility. When early Christians attempted to stop the baking of these sweets, the bakers requested them to be blessed and decorated the buns with a cross of frosting, making them a symbol of Christianity. In Italy, bakers prepare "tortona." It is a bread made from twisting sweet dough around a colored egg and baking it on Easter morning.

Hot-cross buns can easily be made in your classroom by using prepared dinner rolls from your grocery store's freezer. After baking, have the children decorate the buns with crosses of vanilla frosting and raisins.

Easter Activities!

HATCHING INCUBATOR CHICKS

Begin by renting an incubator and purchasing fertile eggs from a local farmer or feed store. Mark each of your fertilized eggs with an "X" on one side and an "O" on the other. Carefully place your eggs in the incubator.

Set the temperature of the incubator at 98° to 100° for the first two weeks. After that, the temperature should stay between 90° to 94°. Turn your eggs every 24 hours, at the same time each day including weekends. Make sure you always wash your hands before handling the eggs.

Moisten the eggs by placing a warm moist towel over the eggs for a few minutes each day. Discontinue the moist towel after day 19. The chicks will hatch sometime between day 21 and 24. Do not help the chicks out of the eggs.

The chicks should not be fed for the first 12 hours. Warm water and baby chick mash, purchased from a feed store, should then be given to them. Keep the incubator at an even temperature, even after the chicks are hatched. Continue to keep the glass cover over the incubator. Open it slightly as the chicks become more mature.

"EGGS-ACTLY" MATH

Twelve plastic eggs (which come apart) and an empty egg carton make this math activity.

Number each egg from 1 to 12. Place one or more coins in each egg. Place the eggs in the carton. Children select one egg and count the value of the coins inside. They write their answers on a sheet of paper, identifying each answer with the appropriate number. Provide an answer key for children to check their work.

CREATIVE WRITING EGGS

Children will love creative writing assignments when they are presented in such a fun way!

Place creative writing ideas, written on strips of paper, in a dozen or more plastic Easter eggs. Here are some suggestions:

The hen that laid a fifty pound egg!
The rooster that forgot how to crow!
The chicken that thought she was a dog!
A chicken took roost in our attic!
The hen that laid colored eggs!
Farmer Brown and his talking chicken!
The chicken that was allergic to feathers!
The hen that laid the square egg!

HEN AND CHICKS

Choose one student to be the "mother hen." The mother hen stands at the front of the classroom with his or her back turned.

Ask all students to place their heads on their desks with their arms folded. They should hide their mouths. Silently tap three students on the shoulder. These students become the "chicks."

When everyone is set, ask the mother hen to turn around and "cluck" to the chicks. With their heads down, the three chicks reply with "peep, peep." (All other students remain quiet.)

The mother hen listens to the reply and names the students who could be the chicks. If she (or he) is correct, that student plays another round. If the mother hen is incorrect, choose another student to become the "mother hen."

Easter Crafts!

MILK JUG BUNNY BASKET

Cut a one-gallon plastic milk jug, as shown in the illustration. Bend and shape the ears. Glue on paper inserts and eyes. A pink cotton ball can be glued in place for its nose and a white one for the tail. Add a pink yarn mouth and pipe cleaner whiskers. Fill your completed bunny basket with Easter grass and begin collecting eggs!

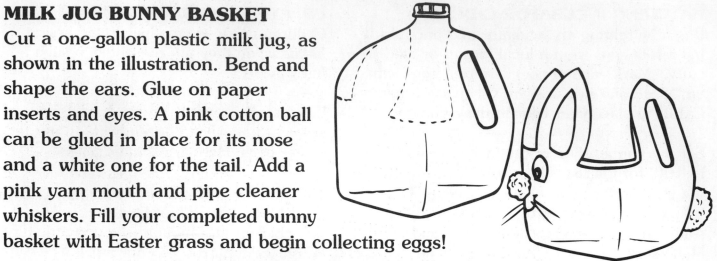

PAPERBAG BUNNY

A small paper lunchbag works great when making this Paperbag Bunny!

Cut the bag, as shown in the illustration, to form the ears and handles. Bend the handle sections together and staple in place. Draw a cute bunny face to the front of the bag and add drinking straws for whiskers.

Take your Paperbag Bunny on your next Easter egg hunt!

EASTER CHICKS

In a small paper bag, combine one teaspoon of yellow powdered tempera paint and two teaspoons of baby powder. Place two cotton balls in the bag and shake gently. Carefully remove the cotton balls, shaking off the excess. Place the cotton balls into the clean half-shells of an egg. Cut two small beaks from orange construction paper. Black paper eyes can be made with a hole punch. Glue the beaks and eyes to the cotton balls to make two cute and easy baby chicks!

Bunny Pattern

Cut this bunny pattern from white paper. Paste it to a folded sheet of construction paper to make an Easter card. Fold the bunny's ears and tail, as shown. Easter messages can be written beneath the folded ears and tail.

FOLD

FOLD

Add pipe cleaners to put whiskers on this bunny.

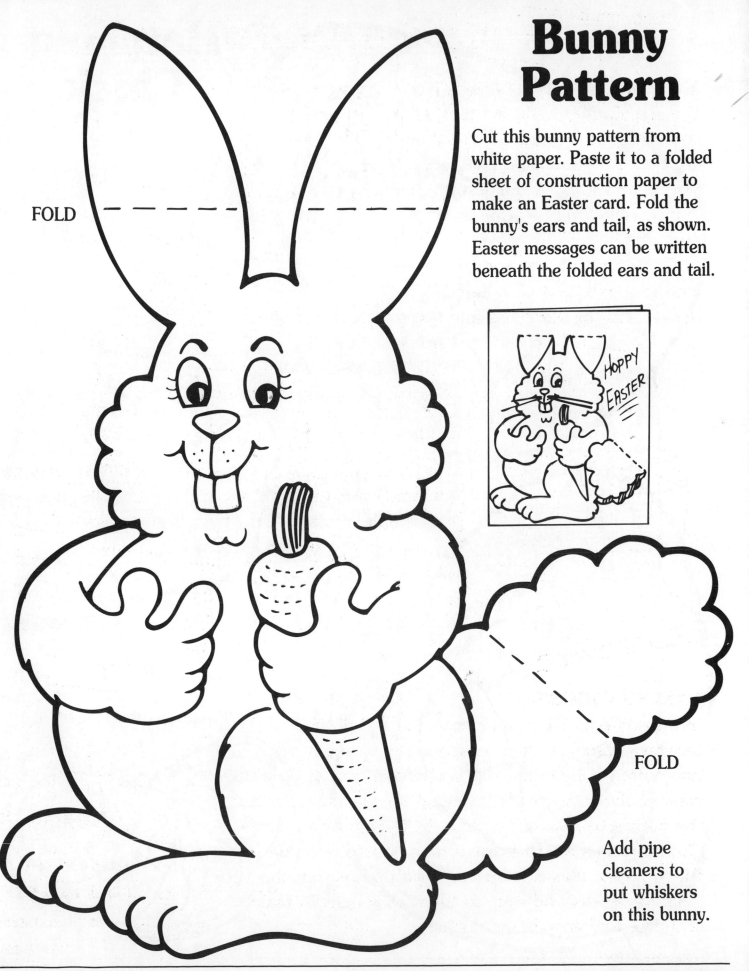

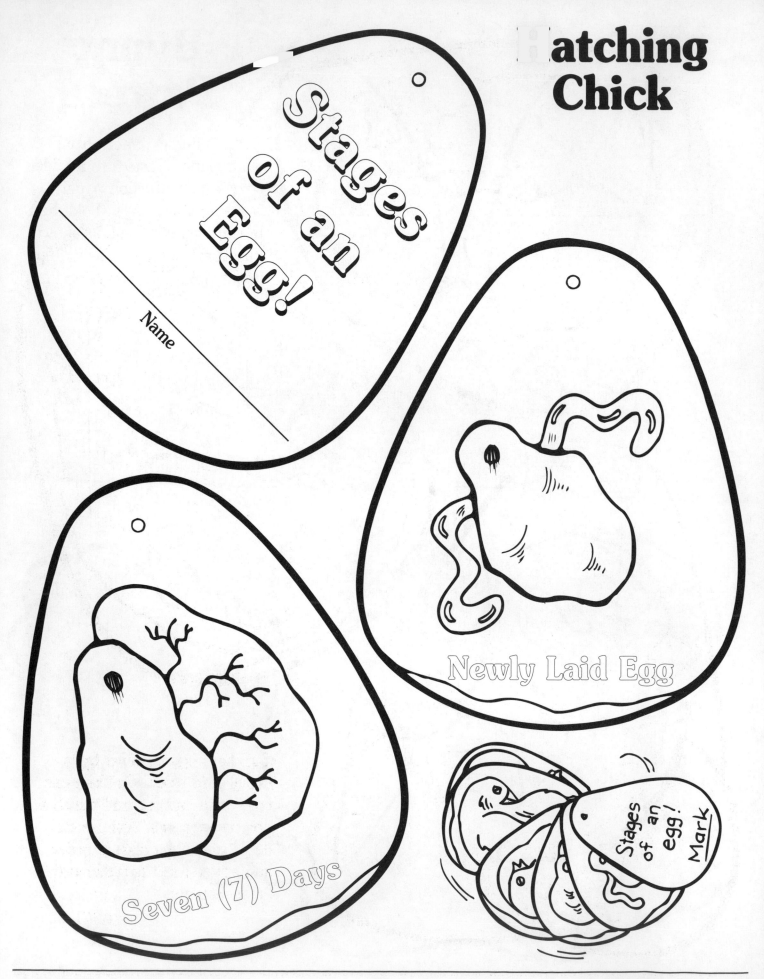

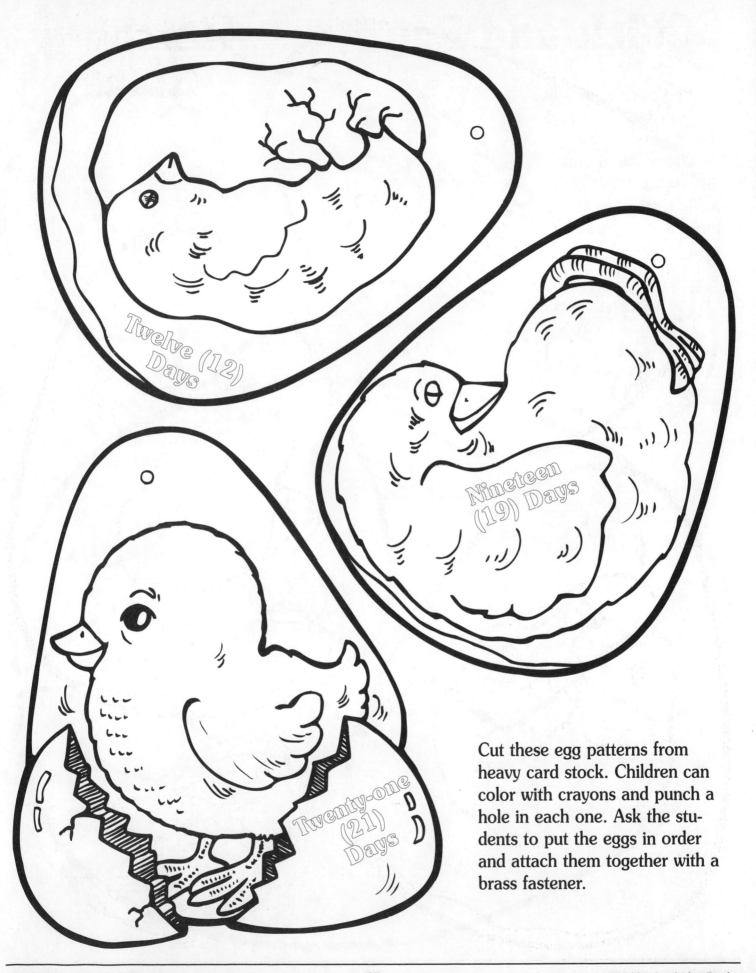

Twelve (12) Days

Nineteen (19) Days

Twenty-one (21) Days

Cut these egg patterns from heavy card stock. Children can color with crayons and punch a hole in each one. Ask the students to put the eggs in order and attach them together with a brass fastener.

Chick and Egg

Cut the chick from yellow construction paper and the egg from white. Assemble with a brass fastener. Use this craft to study math facts or make a spring greeting card.

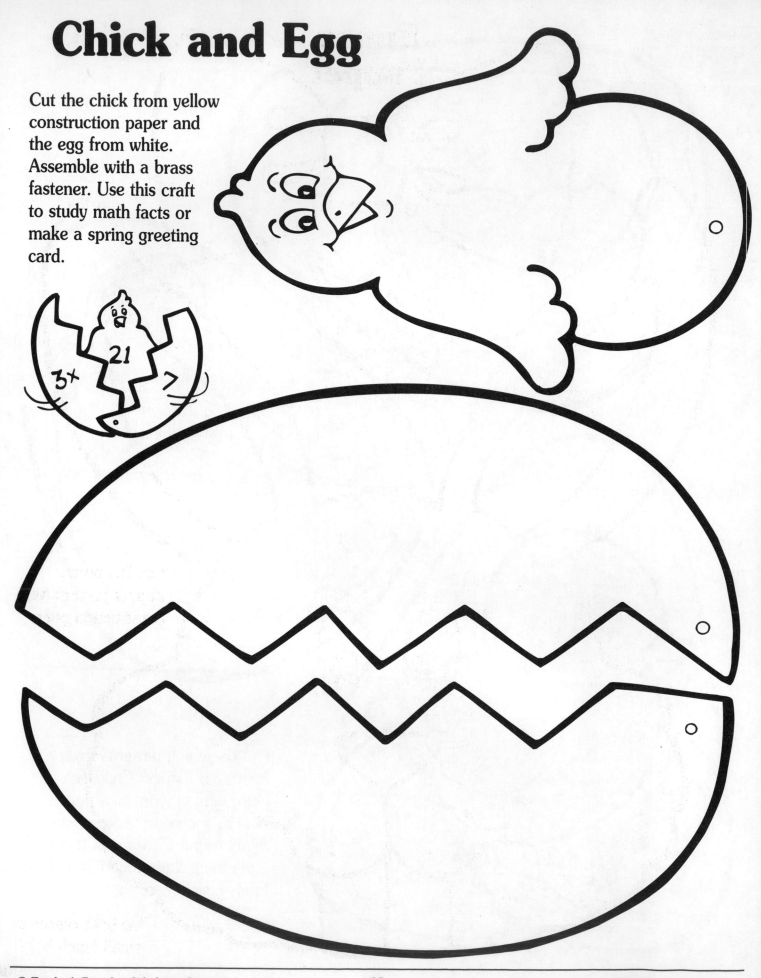

Bunny Puppet

Cut this bunny puppet pattern from construction paper.

Glue both pieces to a small lunch bag.

TF0400 April Idea Book

Chicken or the Egg!

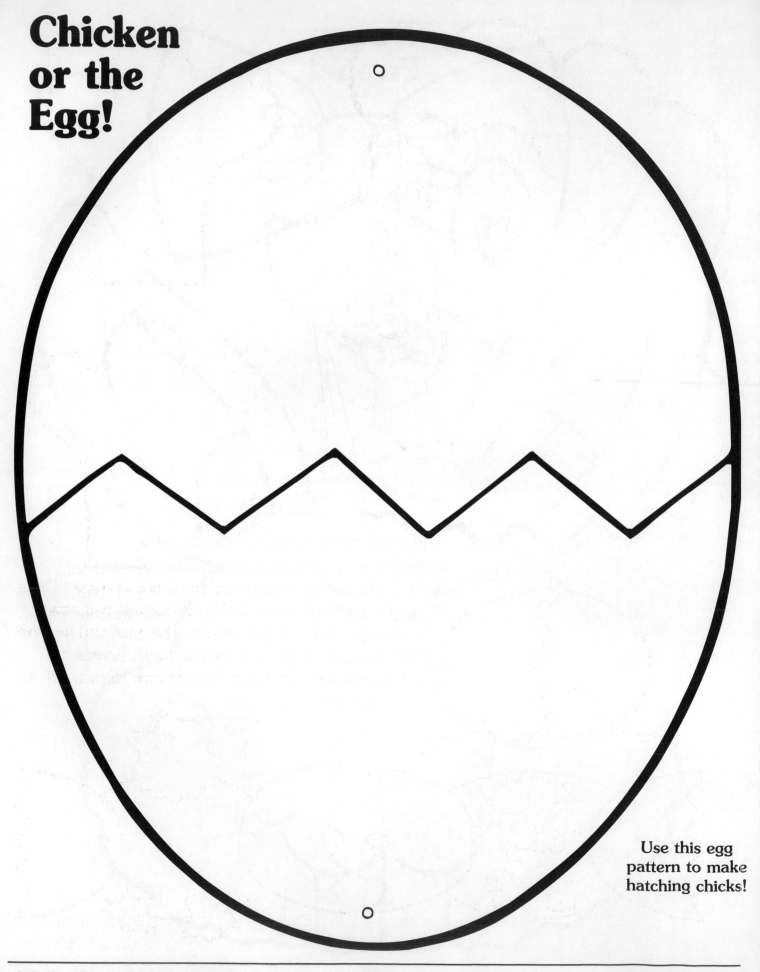

Use this egg pattern to make hatching chicks!

TF0400 April Idea Book

Chick

This delightful chick hatches from its own paper egg. Cut two egg shapes from yellow construction paper. Cut a jagged crack down the middle of one egg and attach brass paper fasteners, as shown. The head and feet are also cut from paper and attached with fasteners. Children will love hatching their own chick over and over!

Bunny Wheel

Copy the "Easter Bunny" wheel onto heavy index paper. Color, cut out and assemble with brass fasteners. Cut out the two boxes as shown.

Cut
Out

Cut
Out

Move the basket to reveal the correct answer.

Add your own math problems or word contractions to the wheel.

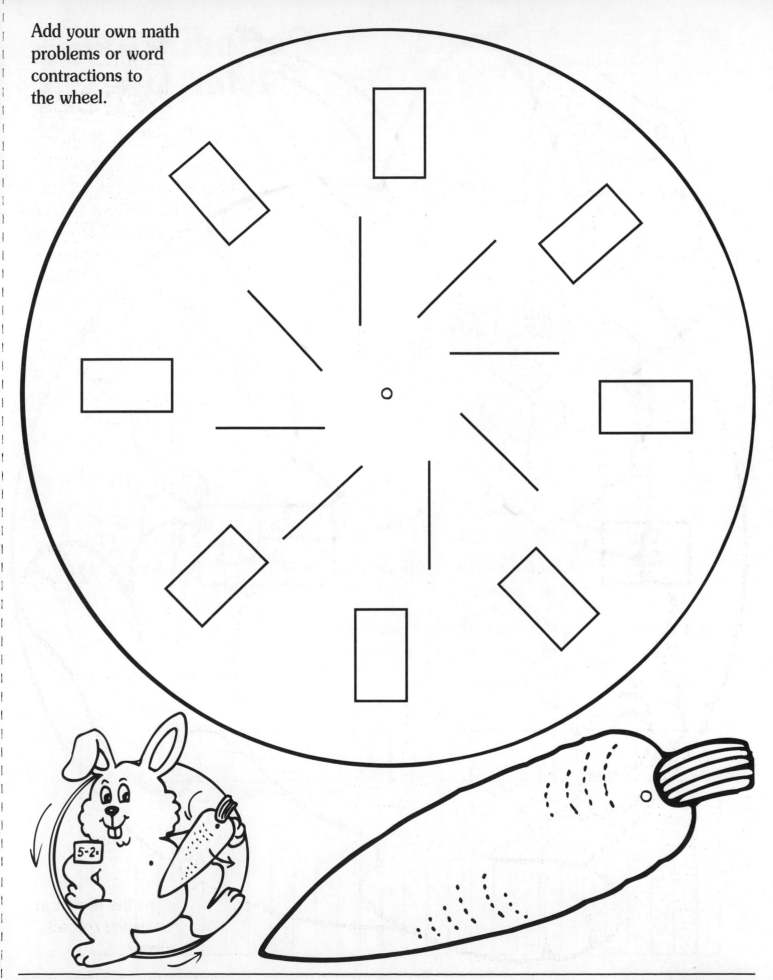

Daffodils and Easter Lilies

Daffodil Petals

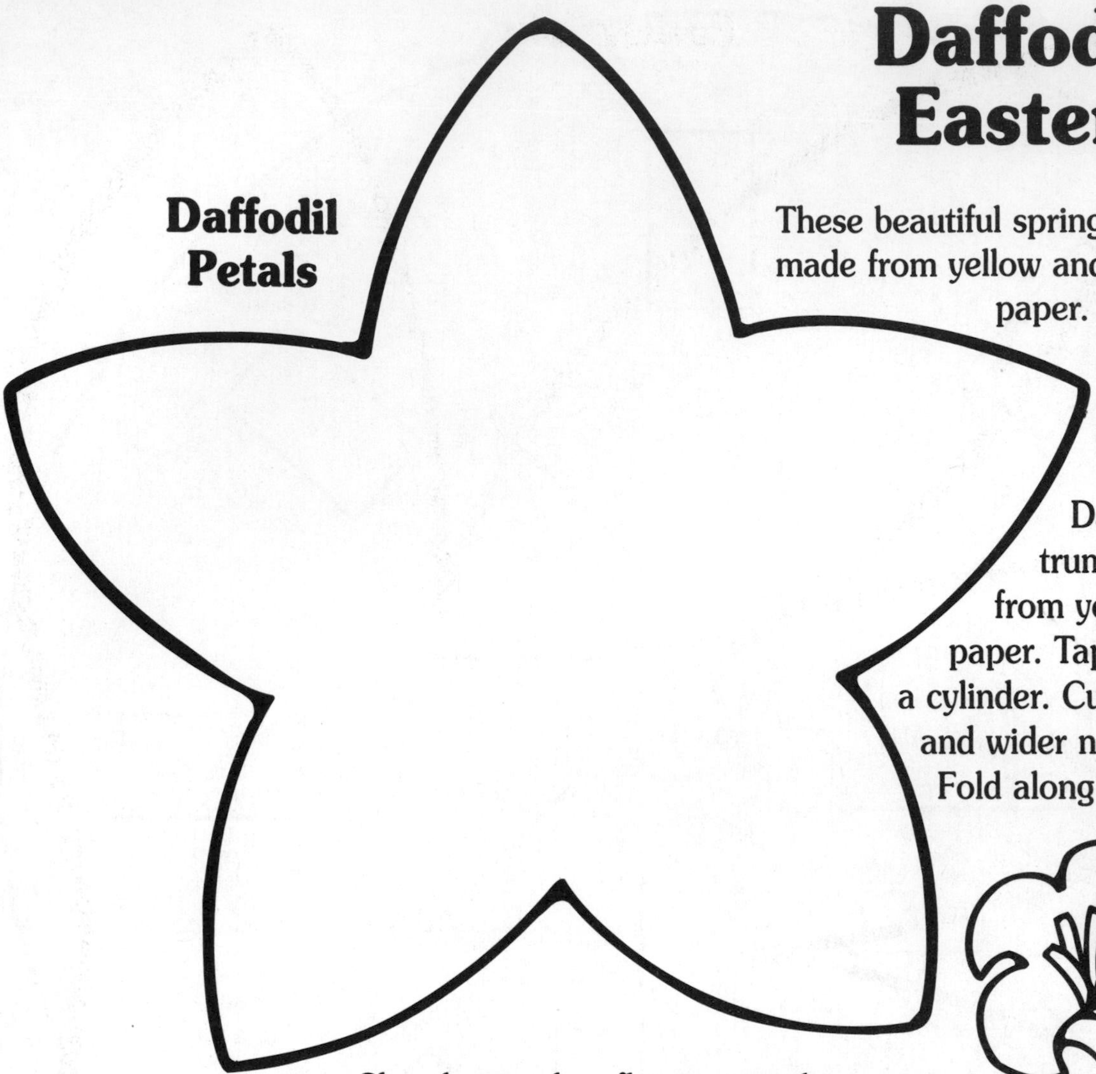

These beautiful spring flowers are easily made from yellow and white construction paper. Pin them on a bulletin board or let children take them home as Easter gifts.

Daffodil - Cut both the trumpet and petal patterns from yellow construction paper. Tape the trumpet to form a cylinder. Cut fringe along one side and wider notches along the other. Fold along the dotted lines.

Glue the notches flat against the center of the petals.

Attach the daffodils to the class bulletin board and add green paper stems and leaves.

Trumpet Pattern

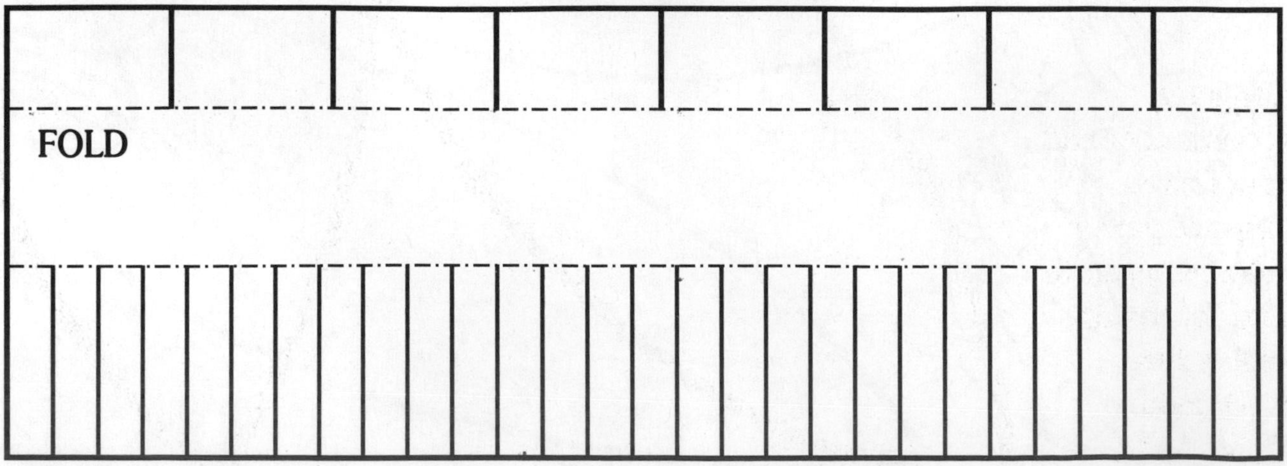

FOLD

Easter Lily

Cut the lily pattern from white construction paper. Form the petals by rolling each of them around a pencil.

Gently shape the lily into a cone or tunnel shape and tape in place.

Attach a green posterboard stem and cut paper leaves. Thin strips of yellow paper can be glued to the center of the lily to resemble the flower's stamen.

Hopping Bunny!

Spring

Color and cut these two patterns from card stock.

Cut out the circles from the "spring" pattern. Fold like an accordion.

Make a crease down the fold line of the "hopper" pattern. Thread the hopper stem through the holes in the spring. Pull down on the bottom handle of the hopper while holding the lowest notch of the spring. Release the hopper to see the bunny hop!

Hopper

FOLD

Cut Out

Bunny Mask

Copy this mask pattern for each child in class. Cut out the eyes and add string to hold the mask in place. Children may like to use the masks to act out the *Tale of Peter Rabbit* or the story *Rabbit Hill*.

Students may like to curl the rabbit ears around a pencil and curve them forward. Pipe cleaner whiskers can also be added.

Cut Out

Cut Out

TF0400 April Idea Book

Easter Place Cards

FOLD

Happy Easter!

_____
Name

FOLD

"Hoppy" Easter!

_____
Name

Pop-Up Rabbit!

Students will love making this adorable rabbit puppet!

Glue a fringed strip of green construction paper to the outside of a small styrofoam drinking cup. Cut the rabbit from heavy white paper and glue it to an ice cream stick. Place the stick through a slit in the bottom of the cup.

Children will love to hold the cup and slide the stick up and down to make the rabbit come out of his hole.

Easter Word Find!

ACTIVITY 1   FIND THESE EASTER WORDS IN THE PUZZLE BELOW.

RABBIT	GRASS
BASKET	COLORS
EASTER	CANDY
BONNET	FLOWERS
HIDE	SUNDAY
DECORATE	SEARCH
EGGS	GREEN
NEST	DYE
BUNNY	CHOCOLATE
FIND	HOP
HUNT	

```
C G H Y N E S T H J K L O I U Y G F S
S F R T F G R T Y H J U I K L O I U V
G R A S S G E R T Y U I O P J H G N M
C B G T R S D R B U N N Y H Y O T D E
E A S T E R B G Y H J H U N T P R F G
G D G D H J O T Y H J U I K O L P K I
W Y E Y Y R N B A S K E T F R Y G H J
R D E E G B N D E R T F V D C S F R V
A V G T D R E F R T G R E E N F I E W
B C A N D Y T D R F G T H N F R N H U
B F T G H Y C C O L O R S V B N D E R
I S D F G B V F G T Y G Y S U N D A Y
T E T H Y J C V B G Y U H J O P N M F
Z A R B V G T H C H O C O L A T E F T
G R V G H B N M J K H P O I U Y T R D
F C F B N M K I O L I D E C O R A T E
S H F L O W E R S C D G Y H N J U I K
S C V V B N H Y C F E C V B H G T Y U
```

79

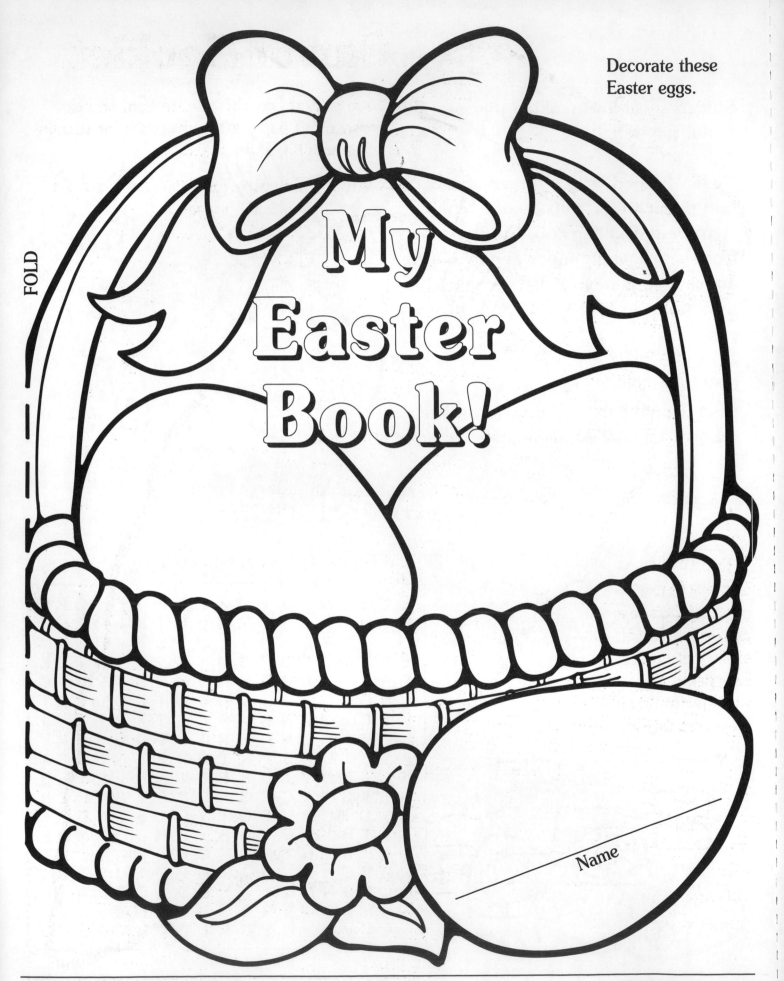

Decorate these Easter eggs.

My Easter Book!

FOLD

Name

TF0400 April Idea Book

Carrot Booklet

FOLD

Name

Have students cut this pattern from orange construction paper and write poems or vocabulary words inside the booklets.

Cover the bottom half of a bulletin board with brown butcher paper.

Cut slits in the paper and place a carrot booklet in each one. Add a blue paper sky and white picket fence for a cute display.

Kim

Lee

Jose

Mary

Mr. Bunny

Display "Mr. Bunny" on the class bulletin board or have each student make their own "Mr. Bunny" character.

As a clever touch, add a fluffy cotton tail!

Hop into Spring! Room 12

Bees, Bugs and Butterflies!

83

Bees, Bugs and Butterflies!

Have your ever walked through a park or meadow on a bright sunny day feeling as if you are the only one around? Well, when we are outdoors we are never alone. There are thousands of tiny animals, called insects, surrounding us at all times. There are more than 800,000 types of insects, with more being discovered all the time! Butterflies, bees and ladybugs are only a few of the more commonly known insects.

All adult insects have three main parts to their bodies--the head, thorax, and abdomen. All insects have antennae as well. Most of them have one or more sets of wings. One way to tell an insect from any other type of animal is to count its legs. Adult insects always have six legs, no more and no less. So we know that spiders are not insects because they have eight legs.

Insects make good pets. They do not require much space and are easy to care for. You can find insects almost anywhere. Look in flowers, on leaves of trees and plants, under bark, stones or logs, and in underground burrows. Sometimes you can find them in your house.

Make an insect cage and catch an insect to observe. Try these feeding tips:.

Ants - drops of honey or bits of raw meat, apples, and bananas
Grasshoppers - fruits and vegetables
Praying Mantis - aphids and fruit flies
Ladybugs and Beetles - aphids, fruits and boiled potatoes
Crickets - raw vegetables, fruit, dog biscuits and crackers
Bees and Butterflies - Should be set free to find flower nectar.

All insects need water. Place a few drops of water on a leaf, inside the cage, daily.

Insect cages can be made from large glass jars and netting material. Oatmeal boxes, covered with a piece of nylon screen work as well.

Always place some grass, leaves or twigs inside your cage for the insects to climb on.

In an insect cage, you can watch your insect's life cycle. Admire its beauty and see how it changes as it grows.

TF0400 April Idea Book

Bees, Bugs and Butterflies!

ANT VILLAGE

Make an ANT VILLAGE by using these simple materials:

- One-gallon glass jar
- One large grocery bag
- A piece of netting or screen
- Large rubber bands
- One small drinking glass
- A shovel
- One ant hill

Follow these easy steps:

1. Find an ant hill on your school grounds or in your back yard.
2. With a shovel, carefully dig up the ant hill and fill half of the jar with dirt.
3. Place a small drinking glass into the opening in the ground caused by the shovel. Ants will scurry around, gathering eggs and larvae, and will fall into the glass.
4. When a number of ants are in the glass, carefully slide them into the gallon jar with the rest of the hill.
5. Fasten the piece of netting over the jar with rubber bands. Place the entire jar in a large grocery bag and do not disturb for at least six hours.
6. The next day, place a small piece of sponge inside the jar. Moisten it occasionally with a weak solution of sugar water. Feed the ants with bread or cookie crumbs or dead insects. (Make sure you do not overfeed them. Remove moldy crumbs with a pair of tweezers.)
7. View your ant village periodically by removing the grocery bag. You will be delighted to watch the ants making new passages, feeding on the crumbs and carrying eggs.

RAISING BUTTERFLIES

You can easily raise butterflies from caterpillars in your classroom. Search for caterpillars in your own yard or local park.
Carefully remove the branch on which you have found the caterpillar, making sure not to drop the the caterpillar. Place the branch in a bottle of water. The bottle must have a small neck. If an open bottle is used, make certain the caterpillar cannot fall into the water and drown. You will need to replace the branch often to replenish the caterpillar's food supply.

Look for the larva of the monarch butterfly on milkweed leaves. Parsley plants or Queen Anne's Lace is home to the black swallowtail butterfly caterpillar. Several moth caterpillars can be found on cherry, willow, oak, apple and other trees. (Make sure to discuss the difference between moths and butterflies with your students.)

                                       TF0400 April Idea Book

Ladybugs!

The ladybug is a very helpful insect. It eats aphids and other pests which destroy crops and plants. In 1888, the ladybug was brought to America from Australia to help save the citrus crops in California. The ladybug is also known by other names such as ladybird beetle and ladyfly. The name "ladybug" is misleading, for not all ladybugs are female.

Like other insects, ladybugs have three parts to their bodies, a head, thorax, and abdomen. They also have a pair of antennae, one mouth and two eyes made of many small lenses. The antennae are used for smell and touch. The ladybug also has six legs and two pairs of wings--an outer pair and a very thin inner pair.

The female ladybug lays about 200 eggs on the undersides of leaves. The eggs hatch into larvae, and each larva hangs upside down to form a chrysalis. At the end of this resting stage, adult ladybugs will emerge. In the winter, ladybugs hibernate from the cold and hide under logs and tree bark.

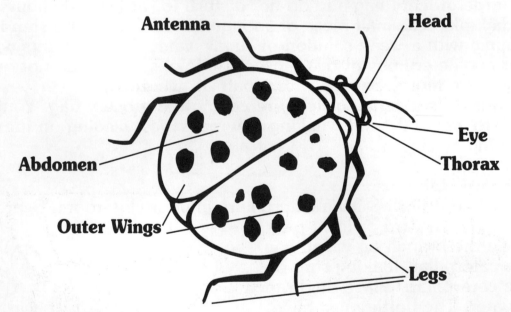

You might like to collect ladybugs and observe them with a magnifying glass. See if you can identify the ladybug's body parts.

Turn the ladybugs on their backs and watch how they turn over. Can you see both sets of wings when the ladybugs fly?

Collect aphids from rose bushes or other plants to feed the ladybugs. You might like to observe the aphids with a magnifying glass. Try to find the larva of a ladybug and watch it change into an adult insect.

Insect Parts

BEETLE

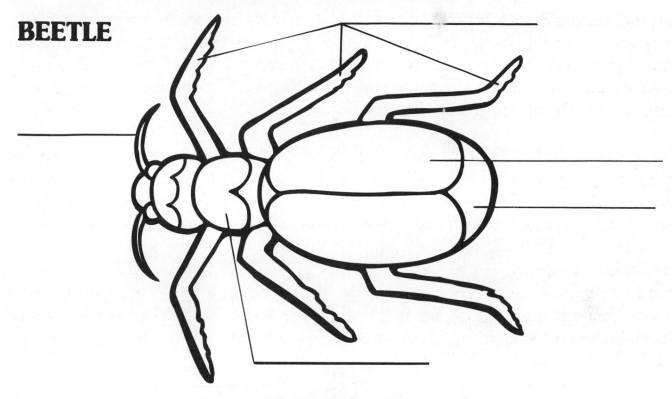

Label these insect parts:

Antennae	**Head**	**Thorax**
Abdomen	**Legs**	**Wings**

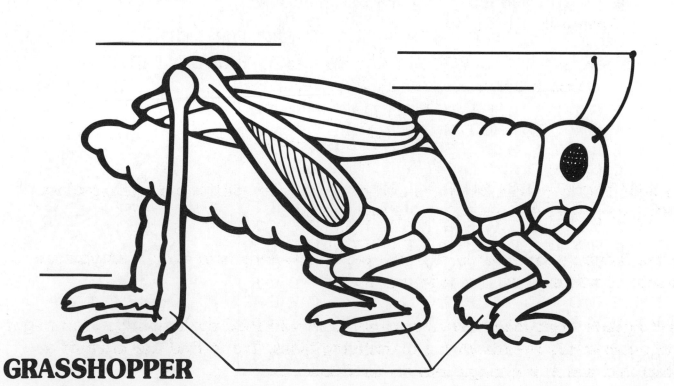

GRASSHOPPER

Insect Puzzles!

INSECT CROSSWORD

FIND THESE INSECTS IN THE CROSSWORD PUZZLE:

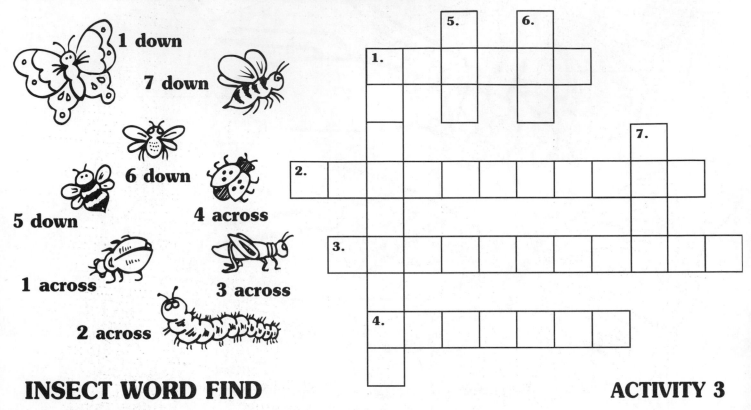

1 down

7 down

6 down

5 down

4 across

1 across

3 across

2 across

INSECT WORD FIND

FIND THESE FOURTEEN INSECTS IN THE PUZZLE BELOW:

ANT, BUTTERFLY, HONEY BEE, WASP, CRICKET, CATERPILLAR, MOTH, GRASSHOPPER, WALKING STICK, MOSQUITO, ROACH, PRAYING MANTIS, KATYDID, LADYBUG

```
C N S D F G T B E R T Y U J K I O L P M O T H
D F G H Y F V U D F G T Y U J U I K L O P M G
M D F C F R T T M G R A S S H O P P E R Y U G
O A N T D G T T D R F G G T Y H J U T O A E T
S E R G T Y H E D C V H O N E Y B E E A D T Y
Q S D F R G B R D F V B N H J M T Y J C D R F
U D F G H Y U F G T W F G T H Y J U U H C V X
I F V G T H Y L A D Y B U G F W Y G H U F I P
T S C W D R F Y D R F E C V K A T Y D I D C D
O W A L K I N G S T I C K S E S F G H Y B V R
C V F T R E C V G N H F T G H P C R I C K E T
A C V B P R A Y I N G M A N T I S B G Y T H J
A C V G T F R E D F T G H Y U J K I L O P N B
Z X C V B N H J M K L C A T E R P I L L A R T
```

Butterfly Mobile

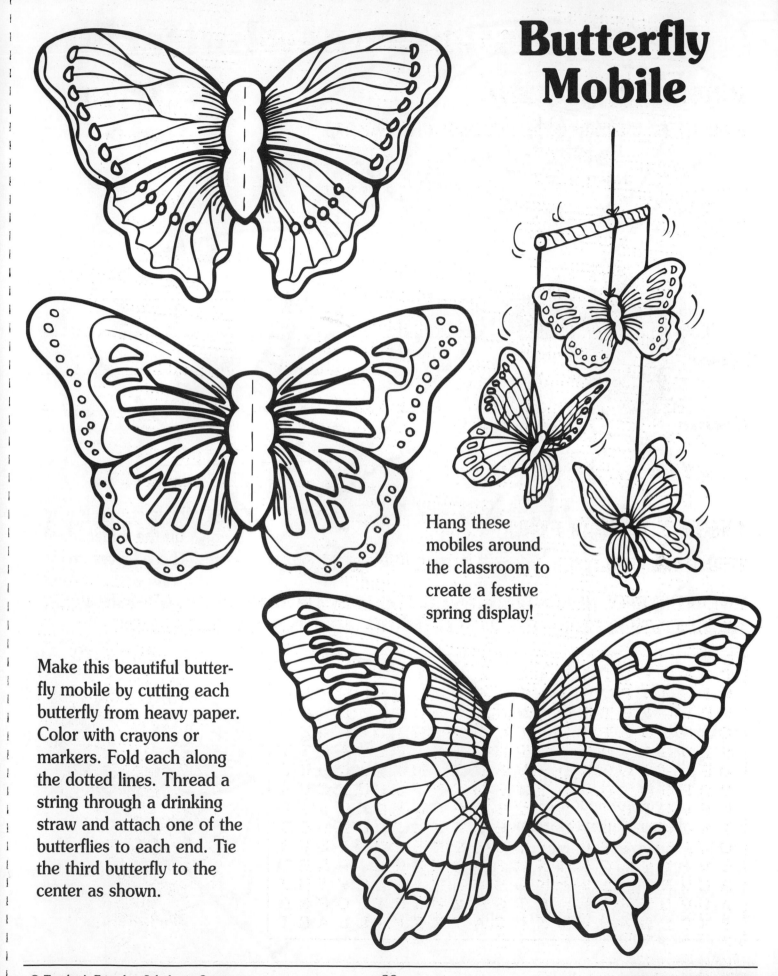

Hang these mobiles around the classroom to create a festive spring display!

Make this beautiful butterfly mobile by cutting each butterfly from heavy paper. Color with crayons or markers. Fold each along the dotted lines. Thread a string through a drinking straw and attach one of the butterflies to each end. Tie the third butterfly to the center as shown.

TF0400 April Idea Book

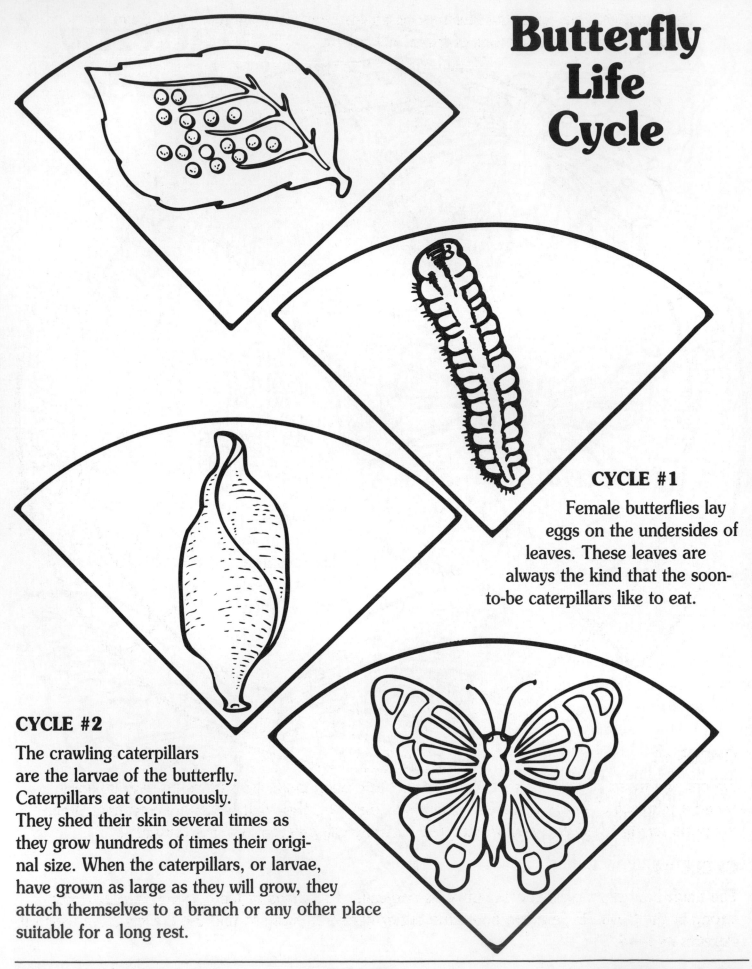

Butterfly Life Cycle

CYCLE #1

Female butterflies lay eggs on the undersides of leaves. These leaves are always the kind that the soon-to-be caterpillars like to eat.

CYCLE #2

The crawling caterpillars are the larvae of the butterfly. Caterpillars eat continuously. They shed their skin several times as they grow hundreds of times their original size. When the caterpillars, or larvae, have grown as large as they will grow, they attach themselves to a branch or any other place suitable for a long rest.

Have students cut apart the illustrations on the previous page and paste them onto the appropriate sections of the wheel below.

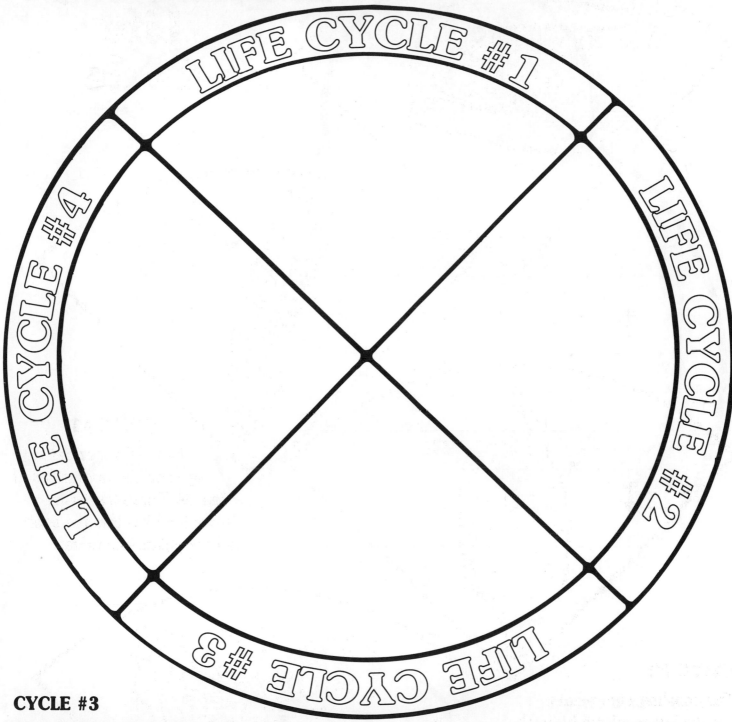

CYCLE #3

We call the insect in this cycle of life a "pupa." The pupa develops a covering over its body called a "chrysalis." Inside this case, during the long rest, the adult butterfly is forming. When the pupa has finished its transformation, a butterfly will emerge from the chrysalis.

CYCLE #4

The adult butterfly slowly comes out of its chrysalis. The wings of the butterfly quickly grow strong in the fresh air. In a few hours the butterfly can fly away to find the flowers from which it extracts its food.

Ladybug Craft

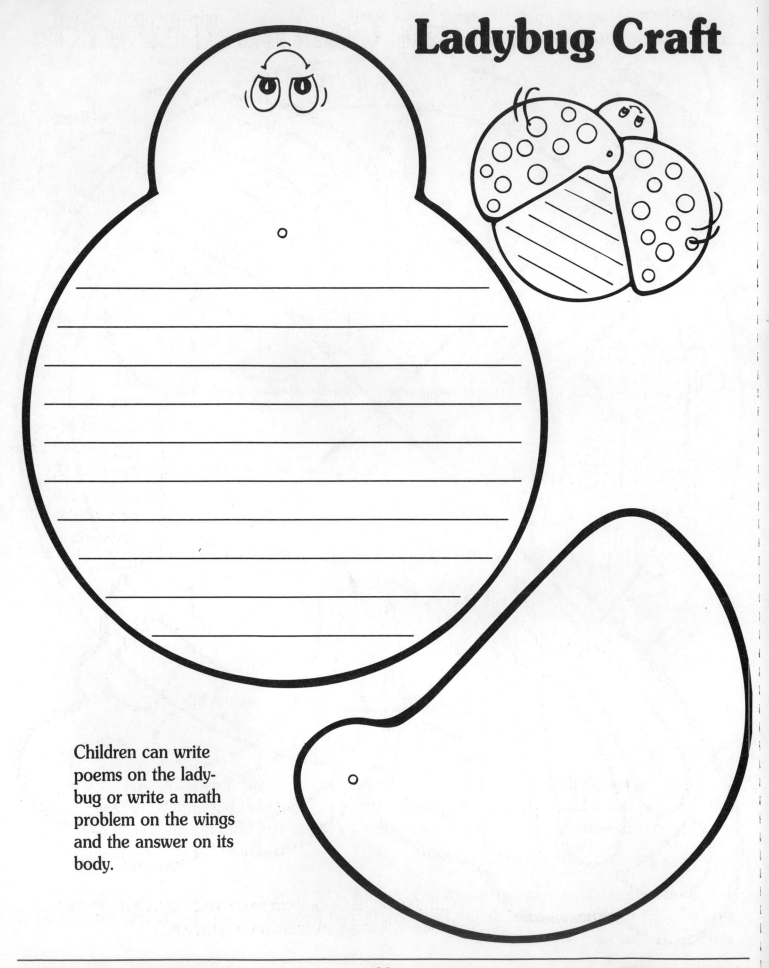

Children can write poems on the ladybug or write a math problem on the wings and the answer on its body.

Egg Carton Butterfly

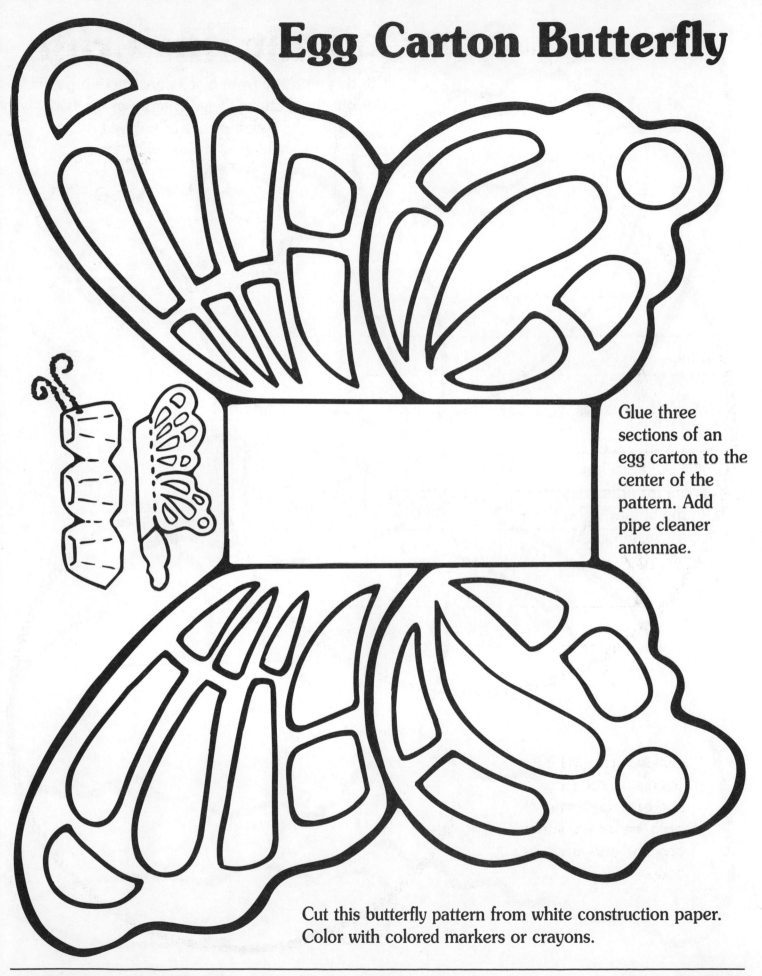

Glue three sections of an egg carton to the center of the pattern. Add pipe cleaner antennae.

Cut this butterfly pattern from white construction paper. Color with colored markers or crayons.

TF0400 April Idea Book

Sun-Catcher Butterfly

Cut this butterfly from black construction paper. Cut out the sections as indicated. On the back side, glue small pieces of colored tissue paper behind each section.

Cut the butterfly's body from brown paper and glue it to the center. Add black pipe cleaners for antennae. Tape the butterflies to the class window for a beautiful display!

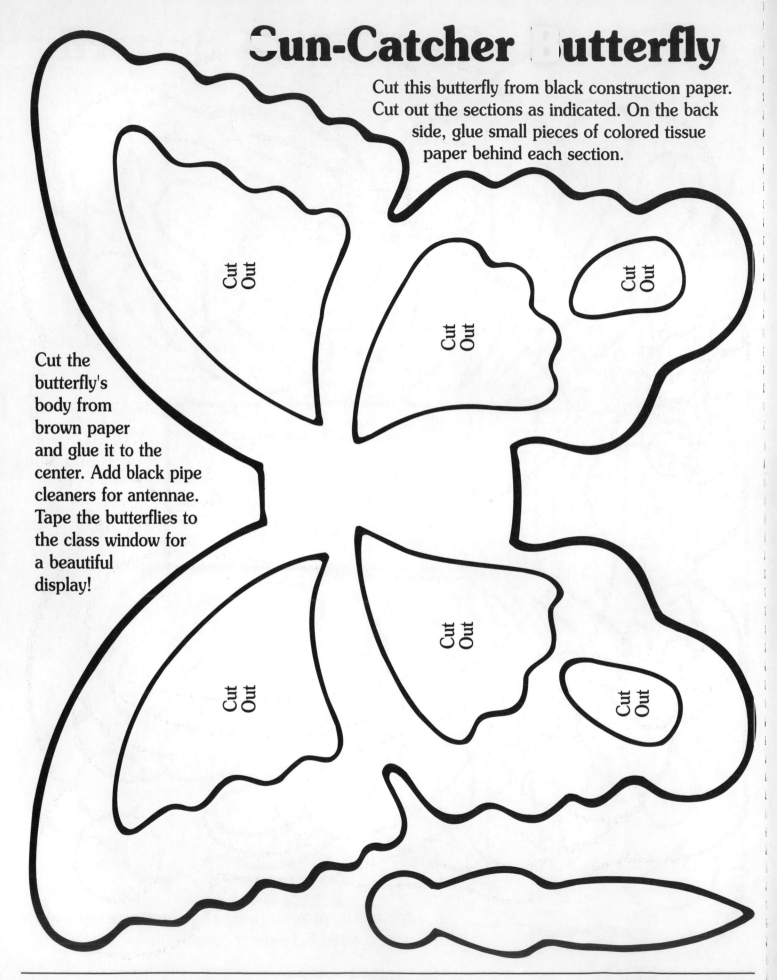

Cut Out

Cut Out

Cut Out

Cut Out

Cut Out

Cut Out

My Butterfly Book!

Name

FOLD

95

"Buggy" Activities!

HELPFUL & HARMFUL INSECTS

Ask students to determine a number of insects they consider to be helpful and/or harmful, and have them describe their reasons why. Here are a few to get you started:

HELPFUL INSECTS

Bees - pollinate plants and make honey.
Praying Mantis - eats insects that harm plants.
Butterflies - beautiful to look at.

HARMFUL INSECTS

Grasshoppers - eat important food crops.
Fleas - spread disease.
Mosquitoes - bite; some can spread disease.

LADYBUG ACTIVITIES

Collect ladybugs and observe them with a magnifying glass. Turn them over on their backs and watch them turn themselves upright.

Collect aphids from rose bushes to feed the ladybugs.

Look at the aphids under the magnifying glass.

When the ladybug flies, can you see two sets of wings?

Find out how the ladybug got its name.

VOCABULARY BEES

Ask your students to write a story or research paper using the following "bee" words:

QUEEN	HIVE
POLLEN	WORKERS
CELLS	WINGS
NECTAR	HONEY
DRONES	SWARM
BLOSSOMS	FLOWERS
ANTENNA	DANCE
FLY	STING
HONEYCOMB	BUZZ
BEEKEEPER	BEE LINE

HONEY BEE QUESTIONS

Have your students research answers to the following honeybee questions:

- How do honeybees gather and carry home nectar?
- How many bees live in a colony?
- What type of work do the worker bees do?
- Why don't the drone bees do any work?
- Why is there only one queen bee in a colony?
- How is a queen bee different from the other bees?
- How do the bees turn the nectar into honey?
- Why do bees make honey?
- How do bees collect pollen?
- How long does a worker bee live?
- How is beeswax made?

"Buggy" Activities!

VISITING ENTOMOLOGIST

Contact your local college, university or museum for an entomologist who can come to your class and share his or her knowledge of insects, including butterflies and moths, with your students.

Ask the entomologist if he or she would bring the various "tools" of the trade along with samples of some of the specimens that have been collected. Many times these specialists are more than happy to share their collections, nets and killing jars. Some may even like to show slides to your students.

After the visit, make sure you have your students write and mail thank you notes in appreciation.

CRICKET THERMOMETERS

We often hear crickets chirp on warm summer evenings. One reason is that they are very sensitive to temperature and chirp faster when the weather is warm. It is believed that a person can determine the temperature by counting the number of times a cricket chirps in one minute.

It is hard to determine when one chirp ends and another begins, so listen carefully. Using a watch with a second hand, count a cricket's chirps during one minute. Now, subtract 40 from this number and divide the answer by four. Add 50 to this number. The answer will give you the temperature in degrees Fahrenheit. Check a thermometer. Were you close? (Don't be too disappointed if your results are not entirely accurate.)

Did you know that only male crickets chirp? Find out how he makes the sound and why.

BUTTERFLY OR MOTH?

Ask your students to research the differences between moths and butterflies. Here is what they should discover:

Butterfly antennae - slender and knobbed
Moth antennae - thick, feather-like

Butterfly body shape - slender
Moth body shape - heavy

Butterfly wings at rest - vertical
Moth wings at rest - horizontal

Butterfly active time - day
Moth active time - night

Your students may like to collect samples that can be displayed in the classroom. Ask the students to try to locate the name of their species and whether it is a butterfly or moth.

BUTTERFLY CYCLES

Conduct an interesting science activity with your class using the life cycles of the butterfly. Butterflies may be captured directly, or raised from caterpillars.

You may want to order The Butterfly Garden. This fantastic kit lets your class see the complete metamorphosis of a live butterfly. It is available at your local school supply store, or you may order directly by contacting the following manufacturer:

The Butterfly Garden
Insect Lore Products
P.O. Box 1535
Shafter, CA 93263

(800) LIVE-BUG

Bee Puppet

Use these patterns to make a bee paperbag puppet or other creepy-crawly character.

You can use the wing patterns on the next page for flying insects or colorful paper plates for extra-long caterpillars.

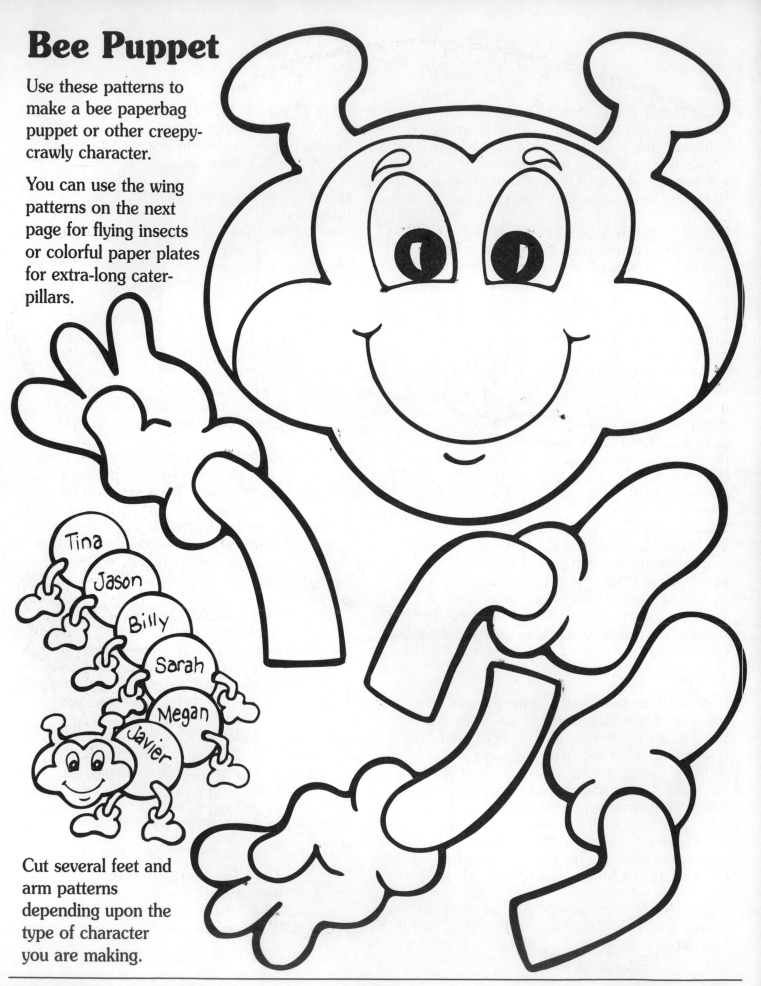

Cut several feet and arm patterns depending upon the type of character you are making.

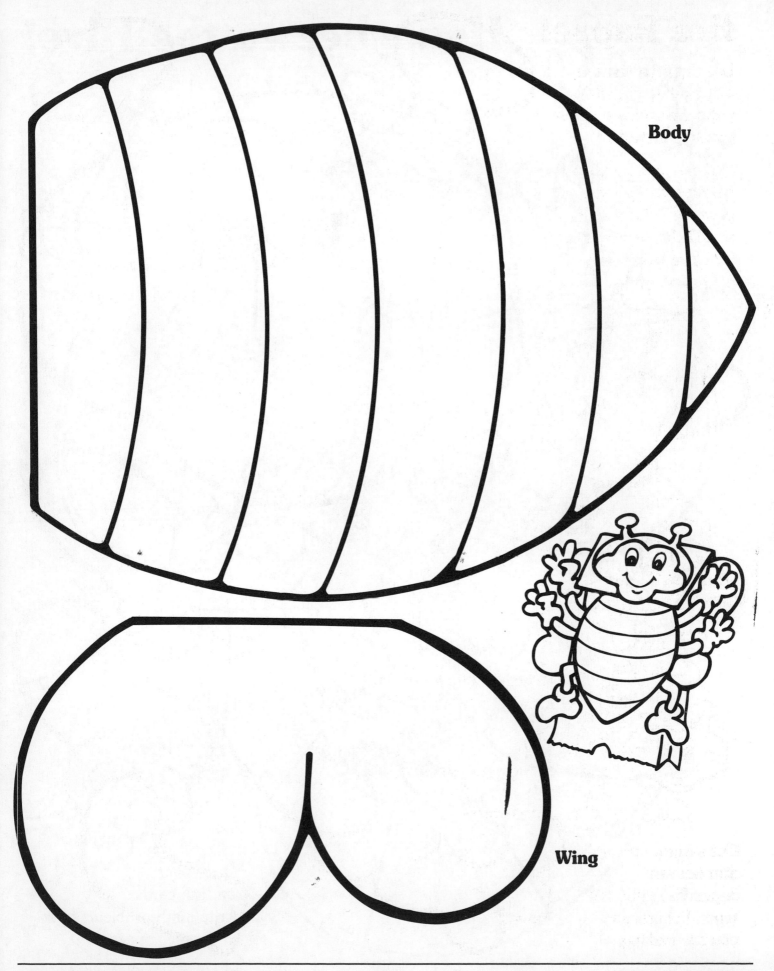

Body

Wing

99

Honeybee to the Hive!

Up to four children can play this game.

Make your own task cards or write math problems to be solved on each space.

TF0400 April Idea Book

Help this bee find its way to the hive!

TF0400 April Idea Book

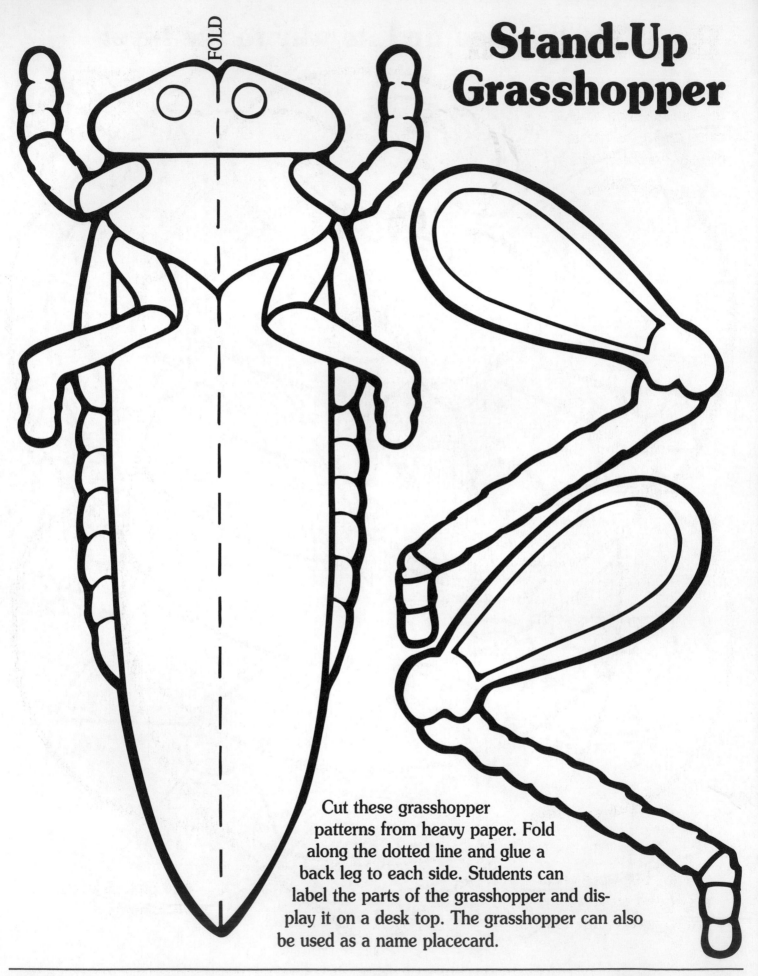

Stand-Up Grasshopper

FOLD

Cut these grasshopper patterns from heavy paper. Fold along the dotted line and glue a back leg to each side. Students can label the parts of the grasshopper and display it on a desk top. The grasshopper can also be used as a name placecard.

Bee Pattern

Make a booklet cover from
this bee pattern or give
each student a bee to
display on the board.

Cut the bee from yellow
paper and color with a
brown and orange crayon.

Add pipe cleaners
for antennae.

Butterfly Color Page

Add your own color code or math problems to the picture for your students.

TF0400 April Idea Book

Fun With Bees!

"BEE" CREATIVE

Assign each of your students one of the words or phrases below and ask them to write a creative story around the theme. (You may wish to discuss these terms in a class discussion prior to giving the assignment.) They may like to use a bumblebee as their main character. Two examples might be:

"The Story of the "Be Patient" Bee That Couldn't Wait For Dinner"

"The "Be Fair" Bee That Had a Hard Time Being a Good Sport"

Be Kind	Be Careful
Be Good	Be Neat
Behave	Be Fair
Be Patient	Be Ready
Believe	Be On Time
Beautiful	Be Thoughtful
Be Brave	Be Smart
Be Gentle	Be Generous
Be Loving	Be Practical
Be Helpful	Be Healthy
Be Lively	Be Original
Be Positive	Be Persistent
Be Safe	Be Responsible

All of these "Bee" attributes are ones we should practice.

"BEE"-HAVIOR BEES!

The theme of bees provides a wonderful way to teach good manners and proper behavior.

Give each child his/her own paper "bee" on which to write a good "bee"-havior. Display a large paper bee hive in the center of the class bulletin board and label it, "We Really Know How to "Bee"-Have!" Pin the bees around the hive for a motivating reminder of appropriate classroom manners.

Here are a few "bee"-haviors you might like to include:

- Always raise your hand before speaking.
- Listen quietly while others are talking.
- Be polite and let others go first.
- Always say please and thank you.
- Always keep your hands to yourself.
- Always be on time.
- Do what you are told promptly.

EGG CARTON BEE CRAFT

Use two joined cardboard egg carton sections to make this cute honeybee craft.

Paint the sections yellow with black stripes. Add pipe cleaner antennae and construction paper wings and stinger.

You can make other egg carton insects. Try your hand at making a ladybug with one egg carton section and red poster paint. Draw black spots with a felt marker.

Three joined egg carton sections make a clever caterpillar craft. Add pipe cleaner antennae and multi-color spots as a final touch.

Name

Date

"Bee"-Havior Bee!

TF0400 April Idea Book

SPELLING BEE CERTIFICATE

awarded to

Name

Date

Teacher

Principal

TF0400 April Idea Book

"Bee" Creative Writing!

TF0400 April Idea Book

My Insect Report!

Student's Name

The insect I've chosen is...

_____

My insect can be found...

_____

_____

My Insect's Appearance!

Size: _____

Color: _____

Number of Legs: _____

Wings: _____

Picture of My Insect!

My insect protects itself by... _____

_____

_____

My insect eats... _____

_____

My insect lives about this long: _____

Interesting facts about my insect! _____

_____

_____

_____

Bug Mobile

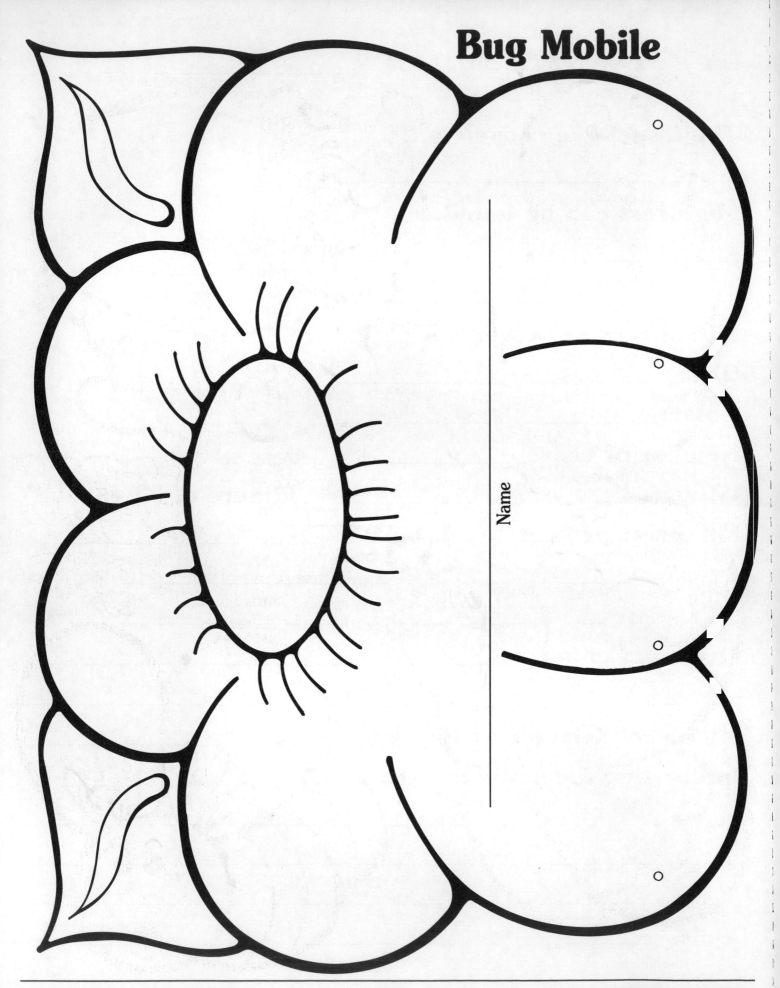

Name

Make this cute "Bug Mobile" by cutting the patterns from construction paper and assembling as shown.

Students can write springtime poems or vocabulary words on the backs of the characters.

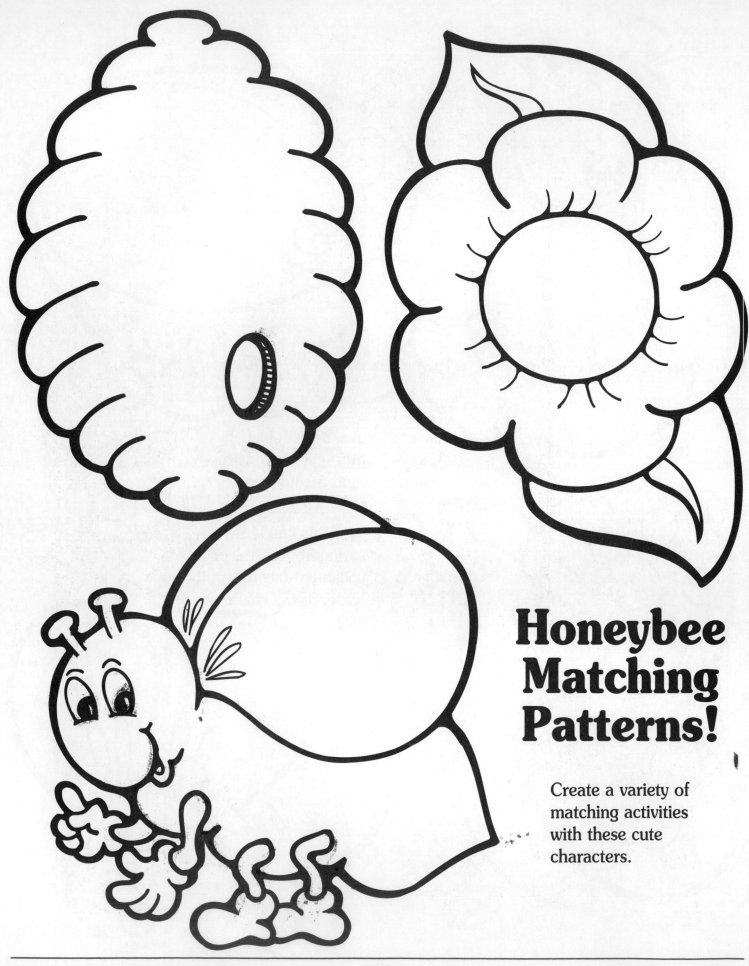

Honeybee Matching Patterns!

Create a variety of matching activities with these cute characters.

The Olympics!

TF0400 April Idea Book

The Olympic Games!

The first known Olympic contest took place at the Stadium of Olympia in ancient Greece in the year 776 B.C. The only contest at the early games was a footrace of about 200 yards. Later, events were added to include jumping, boxing, wrestling, and the javelin throw. Women could not participate in the ancient games. It was not until 1900 A.D. that they were allowed to compete.

In the year 394 A.D., the emperor of Rome abolished the games because many athletes had begun participating for money and had lost their sense of sportsmanship. There were no Olympic Games for more than 1500 years.

In 1875, a Frenchman named Baron Coubertin established the International Olympic Committee and began convincing people that modern Olympic Games, held every four years, would be a good way for athletes and countries to compete and settle differences.

In 1896, Coubertin's dream came true. The first modern Olympic Games were held in Athens, Greece. Now every four years the Olympics are held in a different country, giving everyone a chance to have the games in their own nation.

Today, the Olympic Games come with much excitement and fanfare. The ceremonies and events start long before the actual games. Weeks before, a runner lights a torch in Olympia, Greece. Holding the torch high in one hand, the runner runs toward the country that will be hosting the current games. When the runner can go no farther, he or she passes the torch to another runner who runs as far as he or she can. The last runner enters the hosting stadium, signaling the beginning of the Olympic Games.

Today there are more than 35 sports and 400 different athletic events. Participants from all over the world represent their country in front of millions of television viewers.

At the completion of each Olympic event, the winners are announced during a special ceremony. Medals of gold, silver and bronze are awarded the first, second and third place winners. The first-place winner stands on a high platform as his or her national anthem is played. It is a very special moment for both the winner and the audience.

During the last century, world politics have often interfered with the games. The Olympic Games were cancelled in 1916, 1940 and 1944 due to World War I and World War II. In 1972, a group of terrorists took several Olympic participants hostage, resulting in the deaths of eleven athletes. In 1980, the United States refused to participate in the Moscow Games because of a disagreement with the Soviet Union. Throughout international problems, however, the Olympic Games strives to be a peaceful, uniting force for all countries.

The Olympic Games give people and nations time to set their differences aside and enjoy watching athletes compete in the spirit of brotherhood and sportsmanship.

My Olympic Poem!

O
L
Y
M
P
I
C
S

_____

_____

_____

_____

_____

_____

_____

_____

_____

_____

_____

_____

_____

_____

_____

_____

USE AT LEAST SIX OF THESE OLYMPIC VOCABULARY WORDS IN YOUR POEM.

COMPETITION	ATHLETE	CHAMPION
EVENT	CEREMONY	STADIUM
TORCH	MEDALS	PARTICIPANT
SPORTSMANSHIP	ANTHEM	INTERNATIONAL

International Children
Greece

International Children
Greece

Olympic Games on the Playground!

Have your students compete for "Olympic medals" in a fun and energetic way. Your top athletes will not necessarily be the medal winners with these activities. Here are a few suggestions:

TWENTY-FIVE YARD DASH

Ask each participant to run the twenty-five dash, *backward*! Time each runner with a stopwatch and award the top three winners with a medal.

SHOT PUT

Ask students to throw a softball and see who can throw it the farthest. (You may want them to try to imitate the form of throwing a real shot put.) Award medals to the top three participants.

HIGH JUMP, JUMP, JUMP

Ask each student to jump with a jump rope as many times as possible. The three students with the most jumps before they miss wins the medals.

DISCUS THROW

Have your Olympic champions throw Frisbees or paper plates in place of a discus. (Have the students spin while they are throwing the "discus" in true Olympic form.) The participant who throws the farthest wins the gold medal.

JAVELIN THROW

Provide a box of drinking straws and have your Olympians throw the straw in place of javelins. Have all the students line up behind a chalk line and attempt to throw their straws as far as possible. Award the medals to the champions that throw the "javelins" the farthest!

SWIMMING RELAY

Divide your class into teams of four or five people. Give the first member of each team a full glass of water. (Use plastic cups for safety.) Tell them to run to a given point and back again, giving the glass to the next team member. The fastest team with the fullest glass at the end of the relay wins the gold medal.

HIGH DIVE

Place a bucket at the bottom of the school's slide. Have students take turns climbing the ladder of the slide and releasing three tennis balls at the top. Participants should attempt to get the tennis balls into the bucket. Tell them that form and precision are very important. The students with the most "hits" win the medals.

Olympic Medals!

Cut these Olympic medals from construction paper. Cut yellow paper for gold medals, gray for silver and brown for bronze.

Use yarn or ribbon to hang the medals around the children's necks.

OLYMPIC
ACHIEVEMENT

_____
Name

_____
Date

OLYMPIC
Todd

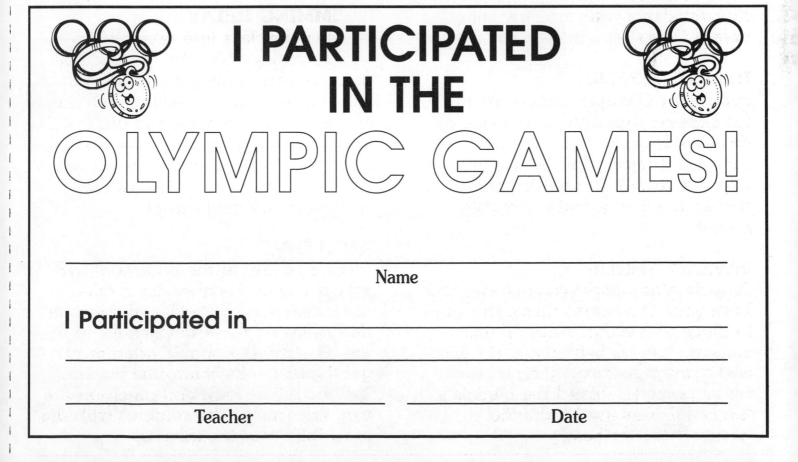

I PARTICIPATED IN THE
OLYMPIC GAMES!

_____
Name

I Participated in_____

_____

_____   _____
Teacher   Date

Olympic Champion Report

I've chosen this Olympic Champion: _____

_____

This champion's sport is... _____

This champion's country is... _____

This champion participated in the Olympics in this year: _____

Some interesting facts about this champion!

_____

_____

_____

_____

_____

_____

This champion won these medals!

_____ _____ _____

Olympic Head Wreath

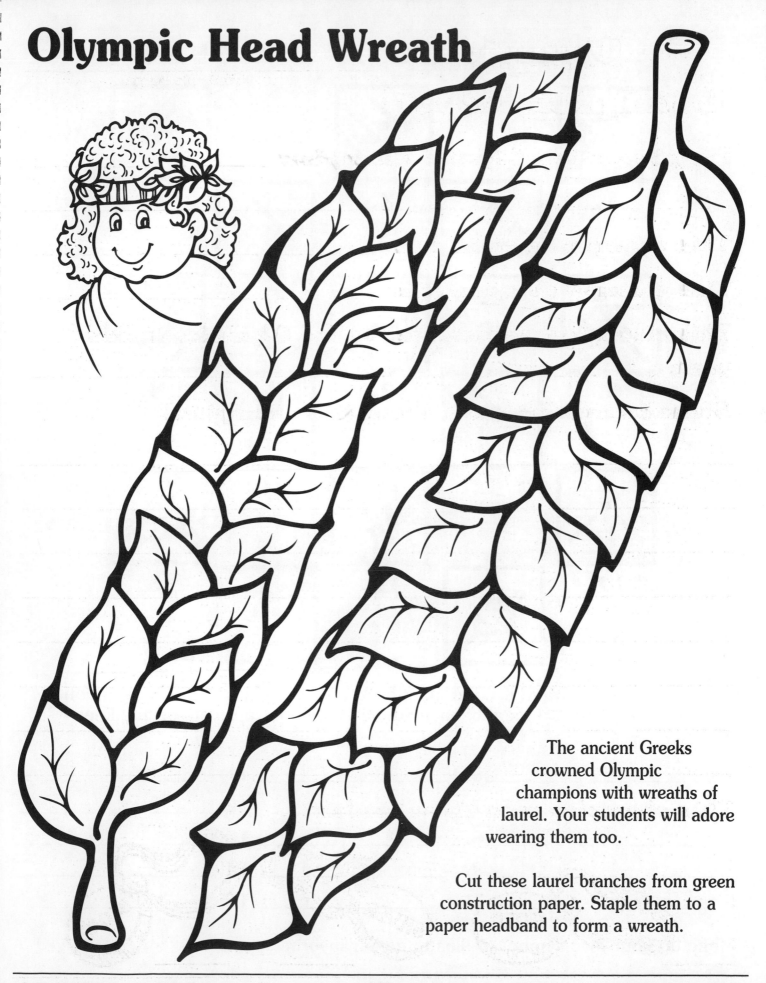

The ancient Greeks crowned Olympic champions with wreaths of laurel. Your students will adore wearing them too.

Cut these laurel branches from green construction paper. Staple them to a paper headband to form a wreath.

Olympic Sport Symbols!

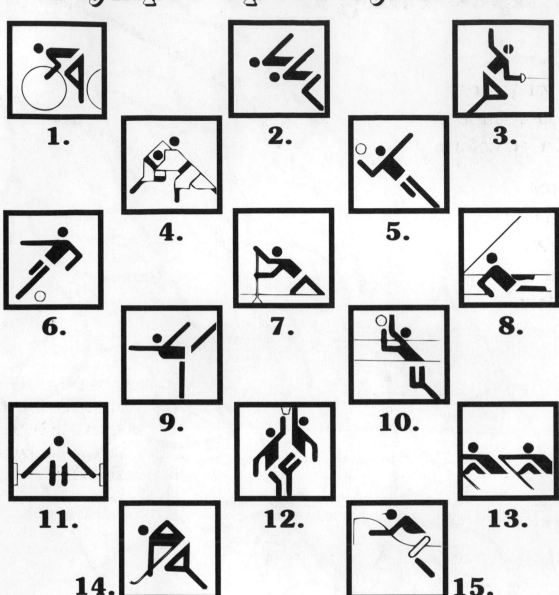

1.
2.
3.
4.
5.
6.
7.
8.
9.
10.
11.
12.
13.
14.
15.

These symbols are often used in identifying various sports during international competitions. Can you identify each sport? Write your answers on the lines below.

1._____   6. _____   11. _____

2._____   7. _____   12. _____

3._____   8. _____   13. _____

4._____   9. _____   14. _____

5._____   10. _____   15. _____

Make up your own symbol to illustrate your favorite sport.   **ACTIVITY 4**

Olympic Rings!

Cut five rings from construction paper in the following colors:

Black
Red
Green
Blue
Yellow

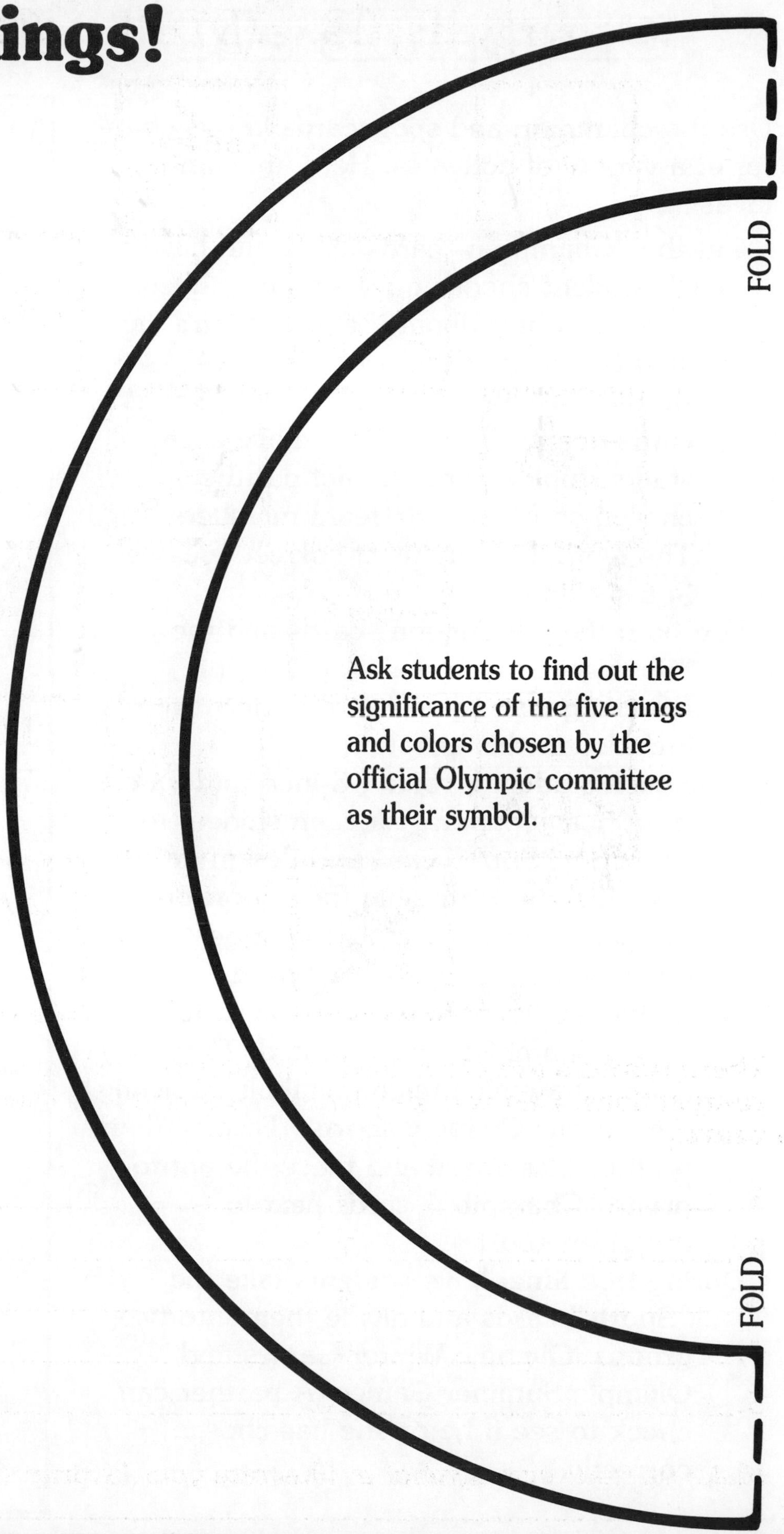

Ask students to find out the significance of the five rings and colors chosen by the official Olympic committee as their symbol.

Pin the rings forming the Olympic symbol to the class bulletin board. Display students' Olympic Champion reports around the rings.

FOLD

FOLD

Champions and Their Sports!

Use the champion and sport cards in this chapter in a variety of activities. Here are some ideas:

- Cut the "Champion" cards apart and have each student choose one. Instruct students to write a report about the champion's life, noting his or her Olympic experience.

- Divide the class into teams. Cut the "Sports" cards apart. Using a timer, have each student pull a card and act out the chosen sport to their team members. The team with the most correct guesses in a set time wins.

- Use both the "Champion" cards and the "Sports" cards to make an Olympic BINGO game. (Bingo card pattern is included in this chapter.)

- Give each student a round, 8-inch pattern cut from heavy paper. Ask each student to choose a "Sport" card and design an Olympic pin portraying their sport on the paper circle. Display the large Olympic pins on the class board.

- Have students identify the sport in which each "Champion" participated. They may like to draw pictures or symbols depicting the various Olympic sports. Display them on the class board and place the appropriate "Champion" cards next to the given sport.

- During free time, have students take the "Sports" cards and divide them into two groups, Olympic Winter Games and Olympic Summer Games. A partner can check to see if he or she has chosen correctly.

GO FOR THE GOLD!

Champions and Their Sports!

WINTER GAMES

Biathlon
Bobsleigh
Curling
Ice Hockey
Luge
Skating
Skiing
Snow Boarding

SUMMER GAMES

Aquatics	Canoe/Kayak	Hockey	Table Tennis
Archery	Cycling	Judo	Taekwondo
Athletics	Equestrian	Modern Pentathlon	Tennis
Badminton	Fencing	Rowing	Triathlon
Baseball	Football	Sailing	Volleyball
Basketball	Gymnastics	Shooting	Weightlifting
Boxing	Handball	Softball	Wrestling

CHAMPIONS AND THEIR SPORTS

Mark Spitz - Swimming
Sugar Ray Leonard - Boxing
Janet Evans - Swimming
Nadia Comanici - Gymnastics
Alfred Oerter - Track and Field
Carl Lewis - Track and Field
Jackie Joyner-Kersee - Track and Field
Elvis Stojko - Figure Skating
Bob Mathias - Track and Field
Edwin Moses - Track and Field
Scott Hamilton - Figure Skating
Frank Shorter - Track and Field
Jesse Owens - Track and Field
Michelle Kwan - Figure Skating

Babe Didrikson - Track and Field
Wilma Rudolph - Track and Field
Dorothy Hamill - Figure Skating
Mary Lou Retton - Gymnastics
Jim Thorpe - Track and Field
Bonnie Blair - Speed Skating
Olga Korbut - Gymnastics
John Weissmuller - Swimming
Peggy Fleming - Figure Skating
Muhammad Ali - Boxing
Dan Jansen - Speed Skating
Bruce Jenner - Track and Field
Micki King - Diving
Picabo Street - Skiing

Olympic Sports Cards!

Boxing	Cycling
Fencing	Judo
Gymnastics	Rowing
Ski Jump	Track and Field Javelin
Equestrian	Archery
Ice Hockey	Speed Skating
Swimming	Diving
Skiing	Bobsled
Track and Field Marathon	Track and Field 100-Meter Race
Tennis	Snowboarding
Weightlifting	Wrestling
Track and Field Hurdles	Basketball
Figure Skating	Luge
Table Tennis	Track and Field High Jump

Olympic Champion Cards!

Mark Spitz	Babe Didrikson
Sugar Ray Leonard	Wilma Rudolph
Janet Evans	Dorothy Hamill
Nadia Comanici	Mary Lou Retton
Alfred Oerter	Jim Thorpe
Carl Lewis	Bonnie Blair
Jackie Joyner-Kersee	Olga Korbut
Elvis Stojko	Johnny Weissmuller
Bob Mathias	Peggy Fleming
Edwin Moses	Muhammad Ali
Scott Hamilton	Dan Jansen
Frank Shorter	Bruce Jenner
Jesse Owens	Micki King
Michelle Kwan	Picabo Street

OLYMPIC GAMES
BINGO

FREE

Olympic Visor

Copy this "Olympic Team" visor onto sturdy index or construction paper. Children can do the coloring.

Punch holes at both ends and attach string elastic or mailing string. (With elastic, students can easily remove the visors without retying.)

I'm a Member
of the
OLYMPIC TEAM!

TF0400 April Idea Book

Olympic Rings Color Page

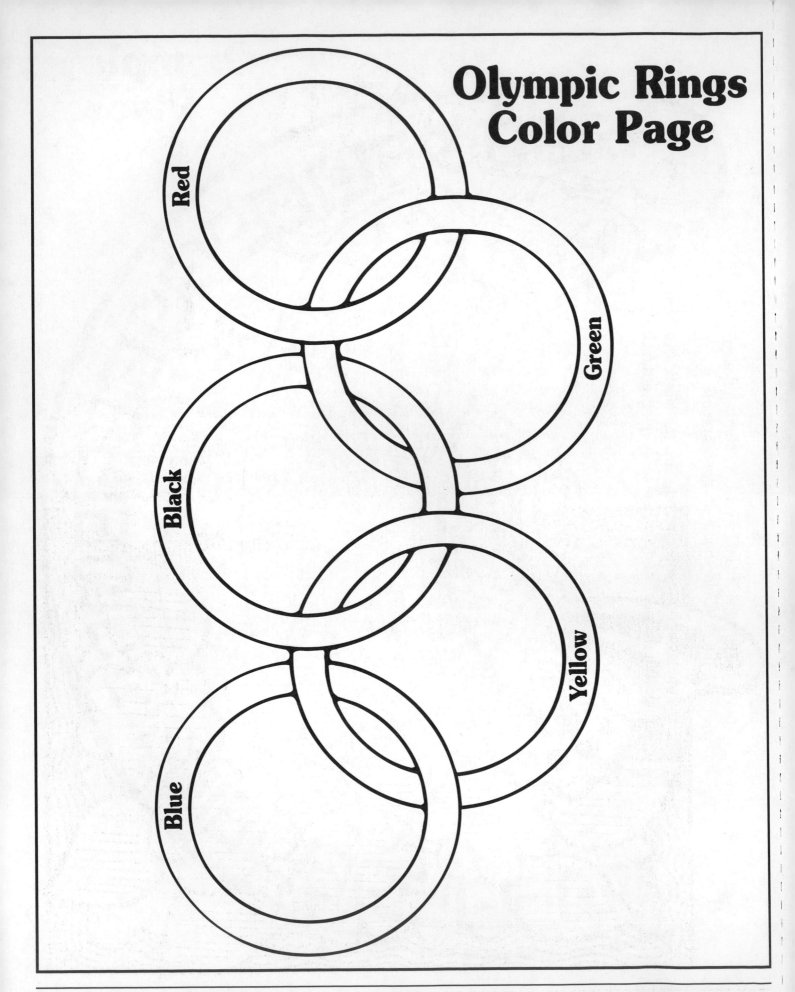

Bulletin Boards and More!

Bulletin Boards and More!

GOOD EGGS!

Give each student a large paper egg pattern. Ask them to show their "egg-citement" by writing an "egg-ceptional" story or poem. Cut the chicken pattern contained in this chapter from heavy paper and display it above the board.

TURN OVER A NEW LEAF

Hang brightly colored flowers around your classroom using this simple idea.

Cut two identical flowers and green leaves from folded construction paper. Glue the two flowers together and add a piece of yarn as a stem. The folded leaves are stapled to the yarn, as shown. Children may write messages about improving behavior with the promise of "turning over a new leaf!!"

OLYMPIC FLAGS

Ask each student to choose a nation participating in the Olympics. Have them draw that country's flag on construction paper and use it as a report cover.

Cut the title "Go for the Gold" from metallic giftwrap. Display the five Olympic rings at the top of the board.

Bulletin Boards and More!

WE'VE GONE BUGGY

Children will love creating their own "big bugs" for this bulletin board.

Use wallpaper samples, giftwrap, foil and newsprint for the different insect parts. Wax paper works especially well for the wings. Display the crawley creatures across a board entitled "We've Gone Buggy!"

SPRINGTIME AWARD TREE!

Cut a large tree from brown butcher paper for the class board. Make sure each student has his or her own tree branch. Cut flowers and leaves from colored paper and place them in large envelopes attached to the board. As a student accomplishes a task or improves behavior, have him or her select a flower or leaf and attach it to the branch.

GREEN THUMBS

Display a large "Thumbs Up" on the class bulletin board. Tint the thumb green with colored chalk.

Research papers on plants or "Green Thumb" awards can be displayed around the board.

Bulletin Boards and More!

BUSY BEES

Each student moves his or her bee one step closer to the hive each time a goal is accomplished.

The bee and hive pattern on page 66 can be used for this cute bulletin board idea.

EXTRA LARGE EASTER BASKET

Students will love filling a large Easter basket with their own Easter egg creations.

Make a large basket using brown or yellow butcher paper. The handle can be formed by twisting crepe paper. Ask each child to color and design the egg on page 140 and place it in the completed basket.

POLLUTION SOLUTIONS!

Let students show their environmental concerns with this "Pollution Solutions" bulletin board. Use the garbage can pattern on page 60 for students to write their own imaginative ideas.

April Showers

March, April & May!

March Winds

May Flowers

Create a perky bulletin board that will last an entire three months with these cute springtime umbrellas.

Enlarge the umbrellas to fit your class bulletin board. List the names of the three months March, April, and May across the top.

Chicken Board Topper!

Cut this cute chicken pattern from colored paper and display it above a door or bulletin board.

TF0400 April Idea Book

Chicken Wings

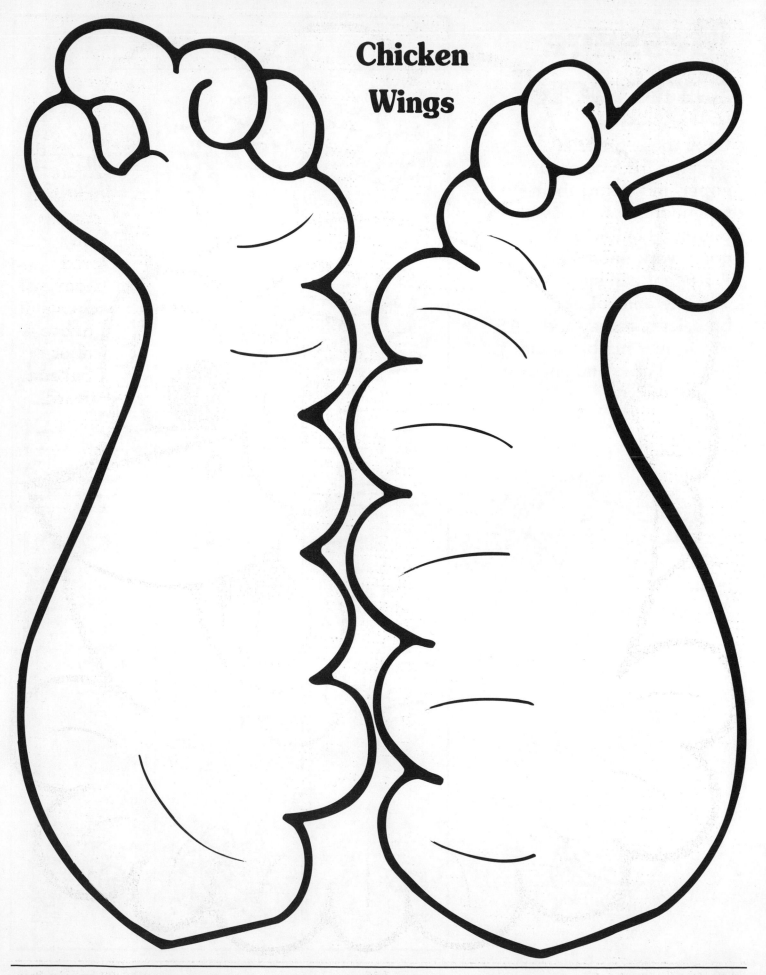

TF0400 April Idea Book

Message Bracelets!

Copy these bracelet patterns from colored paper and award them to students for improved behavior, good work habits, etc. A student can staple or glue the ends of each bracelet together and slip it over his/her hand to take home and show to parents.

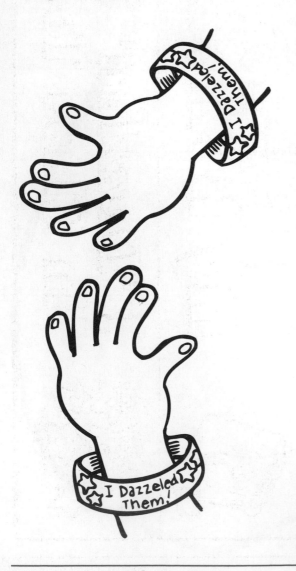

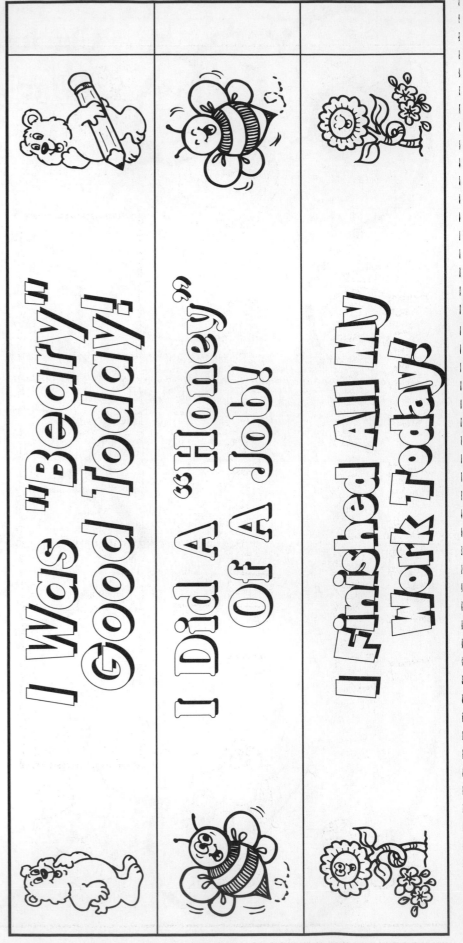

I Was "Beary" Good Today!

I Did A "Honey" Of A Job!

I Finished All My Work Today!

I Was A Good Listener Today!

I "Hopped" to it Today!

I DID IT!

I Turned in My Homework!

I "Dazzled" Them in Class Today!

Decorate An Egg!

TF0400 April Idea Book

Blooming Students!

Cut this flower pattern from colored paper. Have each student fill in the information and paste his or her picture in the center.

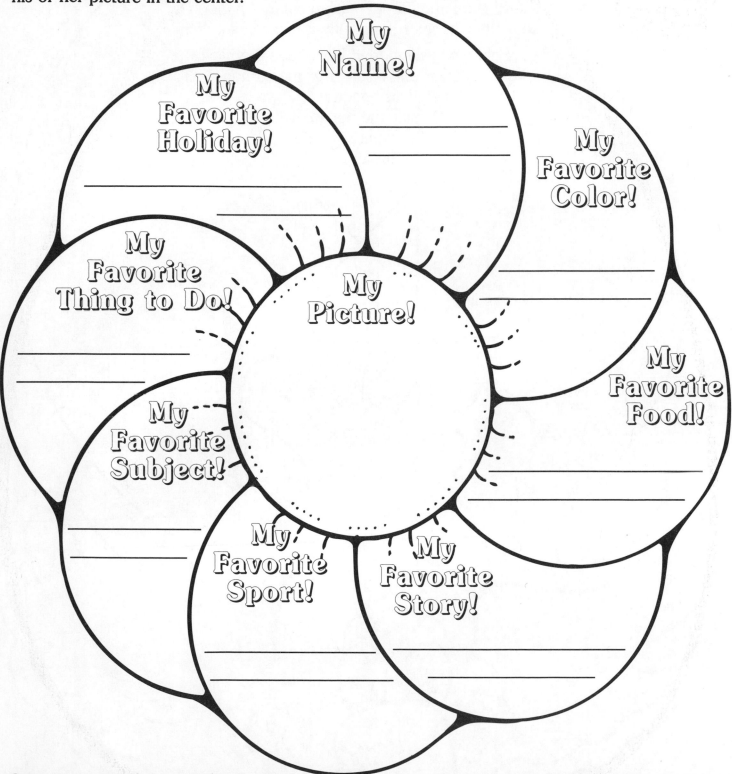

Cut green paper leaves and stems and pin the flowers to the class board with the title "Look Who's Blooming in Class #___!

TF0400 April Idea Book

Bird Paper Topper

Here's a cute way to display students' work!

Cut these Paper Toppers from colored paper. Or students can color them with crayons or markers.

Fold along the dotted lines, tape the back together and insert over the corner of a student's good work paper. Display the papers with the toppers on the class board!

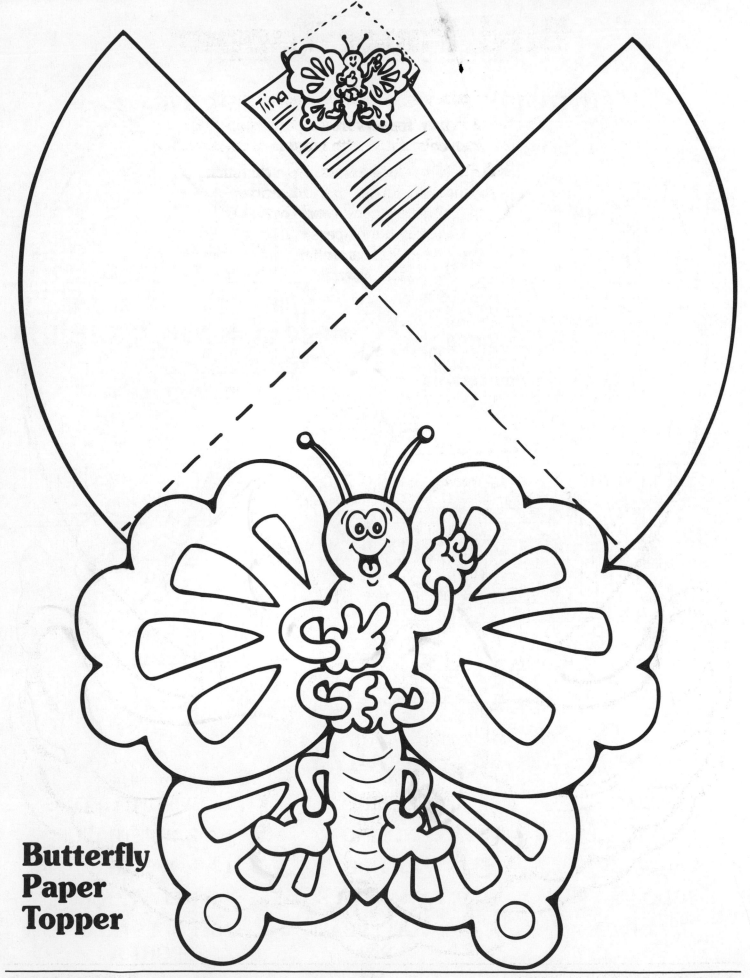

Butterfly Paper Topper

TF0400 April Idea Book

Answer Key!

ACTIVITY 1

```
C G H Y N E S T H J K L O I U Y G F S
S F R T F G R T Y H J U I K L O I U V
G R A S S G E R T Y U I O P J H G N M
C B G T R S D R B U N N Y H Y O T D E
E A S T E R B G Y H J H U N T P R F G
G D G D H J O T Y H J U I K O L P K I
W Y E Y Y R N N D E R T F V D C S F R V
R D E E G B N N D E R T F V D C S F R V
A V G T D R E F R T G R E E N F I E W
B C A N D Y T D R F G T H N F R N H U
B F T G H Y C C O L O R S V B N D E R
I S D F G B V F G T Y G Y S U N D A Y
T E T H Y J C V B G Y U H J O P N M F
Z A R B V G T H C H O C O L A T E F T
G R V G H B N M J K H P O I U Y T R D
F C F B N M K I O L I D E C O R A T E
S H F L O W E R S C D G Y H N J U I K
S C V V B N H Y C F E C V B H G T Y U
```

ACTIVITY 2

		5.B			6.F						
1.B	E	E	T	L	E						
		U			L					7.W	
		T			Y					W	
2.C	A	T	E	R	P	I	L	L	A	R
		E								S	
3.G	R	A	S	S	H	O	P	P	E	R	
		F									
4.L	A	D	Y	B	U	G					
		Y									

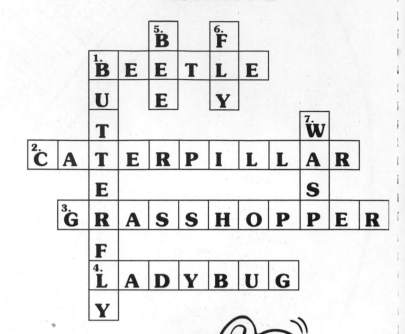

ACTIVITY 3

```
C N S D F G T B E R T Y U J K I O L P M O T H
D F G H Y F V U D F G T Y U J U I K L O P M G
M D F C F R T T M G R A S S H O P P E R Y U G
O A N T D G T T D R F G G T Y H J U T O A E T
S E R G T Y H E D C V H O N E Y B E E A D T Y
Q S D F R G B R D F V B N H J M T Y J C D R F
U D F G H Y U F G T W F G T H Y J U U H C V X
I F V G T H Y L A D Y B U G F W Y G H U F I P
T S C W D R F Y D R F E C V K A T Y D I D C D
O W A L K I N G S T I C K S E S F G H Y B V R
C V F T R E C V G N H F T G H P C R I C K E T
A C V B P R A Y I N G M A N T I S B G Y T H J
A C V G T F R E D F T G H Y U J K I L O P N B
Z X C V B N H J M K L C A T E R P I L L A R T
```

ACTIVITY 4

1. CYCLING
2. SWIMMING
3. FENCING
4. JUDO
5. HANDBALL
6. SOCCER
7. CANOEING
8. YACHTING
9. GYMNASTICS
10. VOLLEYBALL
11. WEIGHTLIFTING
12. BASKETBALL
13. ROWING
14. FIELD HOCKEY
15. EQUESTRIAN SPORTS